Israel 3000 Years

The Jewish People's 3000 Year Presence in Israel

By Jerome R. Verlin

Pavilion Press, Inc.
Philadelphia

Pavilion Press, Inc.
1213 Vine Street
Philadelphia PA 19107
(215) 569-9779
www.pavilionpress.com

Israel 3000 Years:
The Jewish People's 3000 Year Presence in Israel
By Jerome R. Verlin

ISBN: Paperback 1 4145 0692-9
Library of Congress
Cataloging in Publication Data
1. History 2. Israel 3. Mideast
4. Palestine 5. Judaism
Includes index

Composition by Pavilion Press, Inc., Philadelphia PA

"It was, perhaps, inevitable that Zionists should look back to the heroic period of the Maccabees and Bar Cochba, but their real title deeds were written by the less dramatic but equally heroic endurance of those who had maintained a Jewish presence in The Land all through the centuries, and in spite of every discouragement."

Dr. James Parkes, *Whose Land?*
A History of the Peoples of Palestine,
page 266

Comment of the late Herbert Denenberg on the original edition of *Israel 3000 Years*, titled *Homeland:*

In an ideal world, this book, *Homeland,* would not have to be written. That's because the physical presence of the Jewish people for over 3,000 years in Palestine, the unbroken chain of political, historical, biblical and religious connection to their homeland by multiple pronouncements of the international community, make their presence and the principle of their statehood obvious and fundamental beyond contradiction.

But in a world flooded by what the great British historian Paul Johnson calls the mental disease of anti-Semitism and with the historic truth of the connection of the Jewish people to their homeland being questioned by the mainstream media both in the U.S. and abroad, and being called into question by Islamo-fascists, it is necessary to return to historic fundamentals and to clear the record obscured by so much propaganda and misinformation.

So a book like *Homeland* had to be written, and Jerome Verlin has produced exactly that book that is urgently needed. He meticulously documents the great historic tale of over 3,000 years with impressive scholarship and compelling literary skill, all worthy of his important task. In a world that has lost sight of this important piece of history, Verlin provides the reality check necessary for everyone who wants to understand the Arab-Israeli conflict and the historic and moral imperatives that gave rise to the state of Israel.

– Herb Denenberg

The Judean hills, where the first Israelites dwelt c. 1200 BCE (Photo by author)

Late 11th or early 10th century BCE Israelite site Fortress Elah on the Philistine border. © 2008 Foundation Stone, all rights reserved

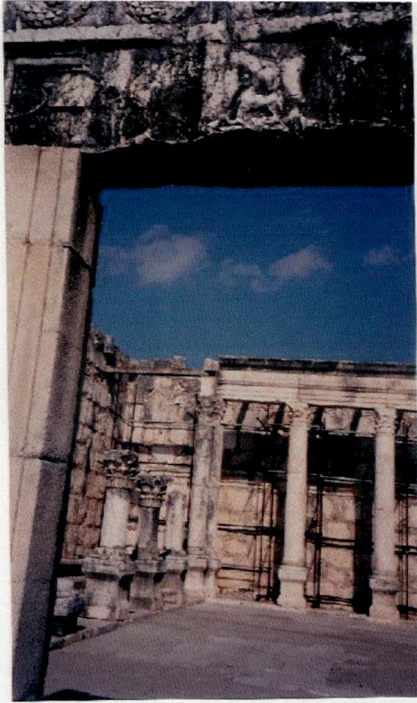

The ancient synagogue at Capernaum. One of many post-Revolt places of Jewish worship and assembly increasing found throughout the Land, evidencing continued vibrant Jewish presence throughout the Roman-Byzantine era. (Photos by author)

Massada from below, showing the serpentine path, and from above, showing a camp of the besieging legions of Rome. The survivors of Jerusalem's and the Temple's destruction in 70 CE held out here for three years. (Photos by author)

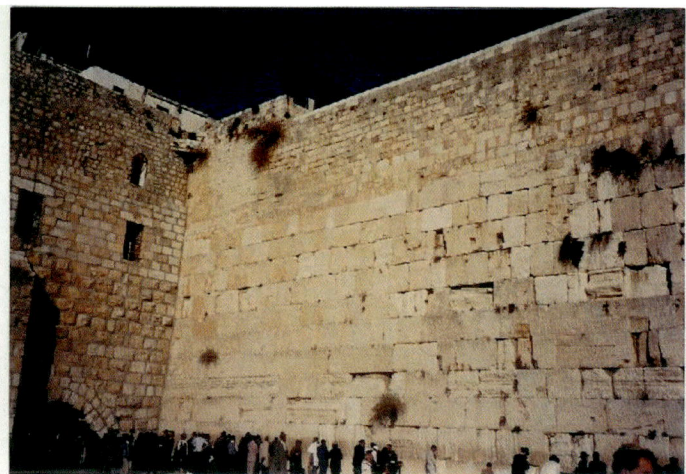

Jerusalem's medieval Ottoman city wall, and the Western
Wall, part of the retaining walls of Herod's Temple, the
holiest site today of Jewish prayer. (Photos by author)

Table of Contents

Preface

Given that the Jewish people, as such, has lived in the land of Israel without interruption for three thousand years, the Jewish sense of homeland is not rooted in persecution of the Jewish diaspora.[1] It is rooted in two different incontrovertible historical facts. First, as proclaimed in the State of Israel's Declaration of Independence: "The Land of Israel was the birthplace of the Jewish people.... Here their spiritual, religious and national identity was formed. Here they achieved independence and created a culture of national and universal significance .... wrote and gave the Bible to the world." Second, following Judaea's final destruction by Rome, the Jews, in eminent historian Parkes' words, heroically endured in the Land, "in spite of every discouragement," all through the long dark Hadrian-to-Herzl foreign rule centuries, writing the Zionists' "real title deeds."

Such a people could not conceive of "homeland" as a place of refuge *that's any place*, however urgent.[2] The Jewish people's sense of homeland is place-specific, Israel-specific. It would not play in Uganda. Indeed, the "Uganda plan's" most vehement opponents were the most persecuted Jews of that era.[3]

---

[1] Compare excerpt from President Obama's 6/4/09 Cairo speech: "... America's strong bonds with Israel are well known. This bond is unbreakable. It is based upon cultural and historical ties, and the recognition that the aspiration for a Jewish homeland is rooted in a tragic history that cannot be denied. Around the world, the Jewish people were persecuted for centuries, and anti-Semitism in Europe culminated in an unprecedented Holocaust. Tomorrow, I will visit Buchenwald ...." "... It is easy to point fingers – for Palestinians to point to the displacement brought by Israel's founding ...."

[2] One recalls Dr. Weitzmann's despair at the world being divided between places Jews could not live and could not enter.

[3] At the sixth Zionist Congress at Basel in 1903, "Herzl announced his new project, the colonization of Uganda, in British East Africa, by virtue of a charter

This book's genesis resides in *what else* historian Parkes wrote in that passage in *Whose Land?* quoted in part in the front of this book. He bitterly criticized Jews for not making their case of their continuous homeland presence to the world. "The omission allowed the anti-Zionist, whether Jewish, Arab or European, to paint an entirely false picture of the wickedness of Jewry in trying to re-establish a two-thousand-year-old claim to the country, indifferent to everything that had happened in the intervening period."[4] Parkes isn't alone. Samuel Katz endorsed Parkes' argument in his classic work *Battleground.* Peters made the continuous presence case in *From Time Immemorial*, as have Israeli premiers Netanyahu, Begin and Sharon.[5]

---

which had been offered to him by the British Government." It was intended as a "Nachtasyl," a temporary refuge in Africa for "the amelioration of the terrible condition of Russian Jewry, for which purpose Zion at that particular moment was unavailable." After deep division manifested by "many stormy and soul-searching scenes" between Uganda supporters and opponents who "protested violently against this attempt to create a 'Zionism without Zion,' the sending of an investigating expedition to Uganda was adopted. "Thereupon, all the opponents of the Uganda project, the so-called 'Neinsager' (the 'Nay-sayers'), mostly Russian Zionists, left the Congress hall in a body." Dubnow, *History of The Jews in Russia and Poland: From the Earliest Times Until the Present Day*, Philadelphia, Jewish Publication Society, 1920 (vol. 3, pp. 84-85)

[4] Parkes, *Whose Land?*, p. 266.

[5] Katz, in his Introduction to *Battleground* (pp. xv-xvi), acknowledging Parkes, assessed that "the gap between what is generally known and the facts of **the continuity of Jewish life in Palestine since the destruction of the Second Temple**" is an "astonishing area of Jewish neglect." Then Prime Minister Begin wrote in his Foreword to the second edition of *Battleground* in 1977: "The most moving chapter in the book is that on the continuous Jewish presence in Palestine. I was glad to learn that this particular chapter has been disseminated in special editions in several languages." (emphasis added)

Netanyahu, December 1, 2010: "A few days ago I heard that the Palestinian Information Ministry was publishing a study that claims that the Jewish people has no connection to the Western Wall. . . . It is not only a religious bond, it is as religious and a national bond, a historic link of the highest level that has been going on for thousands of years, and that too is not trivial because there is a test point here. [par.] I say to Abu Mazen to condemn this, denounce the study, turn to your people and tell them: 'There is a Jewish people here, **it has been here for**

The task I set myself in researching and writing this book was to trace the long remarkable saga of the Jewish people's continuous presence in its homeland of Israel, using words that one non-historian layman uses to others. It's indeed a tale, as historian Parkes justifiably called it, of heroic endurance in spite of every discouragement. I hope to have done it some justice.

In a nutshell: Archeologists are divided whether the Jewish people arrived or arose in the Land of Israel, but agree it was in the late second millennium BCE, a long time ago. Here they established their biblical kingdoms with their kings and prophets striding larger than life through the Bible. The Jews' biblical kingdoms fell to the early first millennium BCE's mighty Assyrian and Babylonian empires, but many remained on the land. Within half a century exiles returned. In the place where the Jews' First Temple had stood for four

---

close to 4,000 years, we recognize this people, we recognize their historic bond with this land and this city.'" Israel Prime Minister's Office, "PM Netanyahu's Speech at the 40 Signatures Knesset Discussion," 12/1/10. (emphasis added)

Joan Peters, *From Time Immemorial*, page 83: "The Jewish presence in 'the Holy Land' - at times tenuous - persisted through its bloody history. . . . Buried beneath the propaganda - which has it that Jews 'returned' to the Holy Land after two thousand years of separation, where they found crowds of 'indigenous Palestinian Arabs' - is the bald fact that **the Jews are indigenous people on that land who never left, but who have continuously stayed on their 'Holy Land.'** Not only were there the little-known Oriental Jewish communities in adjacent Arab lands, but there had been an unceasing strain of 'Oriental' or 'Palestinian' Jews in 'Palestine' for millennia" [citing "Palestine Royal Commission Report (London 1937), pp. 2-5, 7, 9, particularly p. 11, para. 23."]. (emphasis added)

Israeli Prime Minister Ariel Sharon to the Foreign Press Corps in Israel, January 11, 2004: "The Jewish people was born as a people 4,000 years ago, and as a matter of fact, never left. There were Jews that never left this country. And that one must understand. . . . For years we talked mostly about security. I think that this approach was a mistake. . . . I think that Israel made a mistake and I include myself in one of those not to speak about the Jewish rights over this country. It's painful. . . . We speak about the history of the Jewish people. And **the Jewish people as Jews have existed for 4,000 years and never left this country**." (emphasis added)

xiv

hundred years, the Jews built their Second Temple, which stood for six hundred. Maccabee-led Jewish forces wrested back renewed Jewish independence from Alexander's Seleucid successors, establishing the Jewish kingdom Judaea, which fought four wars (63 and 37 BCE, 66-70 and 132-135 CE) against Rome.

Evidence extant today of second-to-seventh century Jewish communities and synagogues, religious works including the Mishnah and Palestinian Talmud, and Roman recognition of the Patriarch as head of the homeland Jewish community until the fifth century, all manifest that the Romans did not "exile" Judaea's surviving Jews.[6] Further proof is that self-mustered battalions numbering twenty to twenty-six thousand homeland Jews fought alongside the Jewish autonomy-promising Persian invaders of 614 against the Romans' Byzantine heirs.

We have evidence of homeland Jewish communities throughout the Muslim dynastic era (638-1099), which began as Arab and progressively faded to Turk. The 1099 Crusaders themselves acknowledged that "Turk, Arab and Jew" confronted them at Jerusalem, of whom "the Jew is the last to fall," and that Haifa's Jews courageously held them off for a month.

The Yishuv, the community of the homeland's Jews, endured Crusader rule and the two century rule of the non-Arab Mamluks who followed, and then the four-hundred-year rule of the non-Arab Ottoman Turks after them. They continued to live not only in the Jews' four holy cities of Jerusalem, Safad, Tiberias and Hebron, but as well in the rural grassroots of the land. Jews again became Jerusalem's

---

[6] Contra: Jimmy Carter, *Palestine: Peace Not Apartheid*, New York, Simon & Schuster, 2006, p. 2: "135: Romans suppress a Jewish revolt, killing or forcing almost all Jews of Judaea into exile." Carter's opening "Historical Chronology," from which this dateline is taken, doesn't mention Jews again until 1917.

majority population in pre-Zionist 19th century Ottoman times. It was to an already reviving Yishuv that the Zionists came.

The tale, so far as it is told in this book, concludes with Ben-Gurion, standing beneath Herzl's portrait, re-proclaiming Jewish homeland independence in Israel. But taking a peek beyond that, it was a homeland Jewish army, the Haganah, which became the Israel Defense Force, that threw back and then some the instant invasion of several neighboring states.

That's the tale that's told in this book while you stand on one leg. Come now and read.

Chapter 1
Israelite Origins

1.1 The Great Debate

A book claiming for Jews a continuous three-millennia homeland presence in Israel must take up at the outset how the Israelites, as Jews were originally known, arrived or arose in that land.

Arrived or arose? Some regard very questioning of the Bible unsettling, even heretical, but credentialed Conquest ("arrived" from outside Canaan) believers, e.g., Hoffmeier and Herzog, have addressed the indigenous origins ("arose" from within the Canaanite population) case on the merits. Neither side is wholly convincing. "The origins of Israel," one expert pithily put it, "remain obscure." But "the game is afoot," Holmes would entice us, so come along with me on this deepest of quests for peoplehood roots.

We start with two indigenous origins models – Finkelstein's desert nomadic herders settling down in the hills from the east, and Dever's lowland farmers moving up into the hills from the west. Then we show Hoffmeier arguing for daylight between discredited early "archeology proving the Bible" claims and the Conquest as described in the Bible. In support of biblical "authenticity," we present external evidence supporting two highly detailed accounts in the Bible, biblical battles and Solomon's Temple. Then we trace back into the past two anciently-hallowed possessions of the Jewish people today – their Hebrew Bible and Passover holiday.

For us, the significance of the Conquest versus Indigenous Origins debate resides not in the snipings within or between the two camps, but in both camps' consensus that history takes note of the Jewish people in Israel, whether they arrived or arose there, by the Late Bronze-Iron I Age transition, c. 1200 BCE, a Long time ago.

1.2   The "Indigenous Origins" Case

1.2.1   The Death of Archeological Innocence

Early 20th century archeologists excavated sites identified with the Israelite conquest, "to see," as Israeli archeologist Israel Finkelstein and co-author N.A. Silberman of *The Bible Unearthed* put it, "if any evidence of fallen walls, burnt beams and wholesale destruction could be found."[1] They found Canaanite sites seemingly destroyed in the late 13th century and resettled by a less advanced people. "Thus, for much of the twentieth century," they wrote, "archeology seemed to confirm the Bible's account."

But it became increasingly clear that "many of the most important pieces of the archeological puzzle simply did not fit." In Jericho no trace was found of 13th century BCE settlement, and the earlier 14th century settlement, antedating the Conquest, was small and unfortified, with no sign of destruction. At Ai, where Joshua carried out a clever ambush, a huge Early Bronze Age city was found, but that was a millennium earlier. "Not a single pottery sherd or any other indication of settlement there in the Late Bronze Age was recovered. Renewed excavations at the site in the 1960's produced the same picture." So too at Gibeon, where the sun stood still, Middle Bronze and Iron Age, but no Late Bronze Age remains, were uncovered. And so too elsewhere. And at some destroyed sites, "the destroyers were not necessarily Israelites."[2]

Archeologist William Dever devoted two chapters of his 2003 book *Who Were the Early Israelites and Where Did They Come From?* to archeological objections to the Israelite conquests, first in Transjordan and then in Canaan itself.

---

[1] Finkelstein & Silberman, p. 79
[2] Finkelstein & Silberman, pp. 81-83.

As for the Bible's pre-Canaan actions, Exodus states that the Israelites first considered entering Canaan "by way of the land of the Philistines," but Dever calls this a Bible writers' anachronism, in that the Philistines[3] didn't arrive in Canaan until c. 1180 BCE, well after the consensus time of the Exodus. After their 40-year desert sojourn, mostly at Kadesh-Barnea, the Bible has the Edomites blocking the Israelites' passage through southern Transjorrdan. But "we now know, writes Dever, that occupation of Edom did not begin until much later, and even then it was extremely sparse. And the area remained largely nomadic until perhaps the 7th century B.C., when a sort of semi-sedentary 'tribal state' finally emerged. . . . What this means is that there cannot have been a king of Edom to have denied the Israelites access, since Edom did not achieve any kind of statehood until the 7th century B.C."[4] After citing absence of evidence for other Bible-described Israelite actions on both sides of the Jordan, Dever concludes:

"The foregoing survey of the archeological data leaves one, I think with little choice. We must confront the fact that the external material evidence supports *almost nothing* [italics original] of the biblical account of a large-scale, concerted Israelite military invasion of Canaan . . . ."[5]

1.2.2 Non-Conquest Alternatives

But if not by Conquest, then how? Three models developed:

[1] Israelites as Infiltrating Pastoralists: This Alt-Noth model proposed that outsider Israelites infiltrated mostly peacefully from the desert into sparsely settled eastern hills.[6]

[2] Israelites as Rebelling Canaanite Peasants: Mendenhall and Gottwald's model had downtrodden Canaanite lowland farmers revolt and flee up into the hills, where they evolved into the Israelites. Dever today advocates a revised "peasants' revolt" model.

[3] Israelites as Sedentarizing Canaanite Pastoral Nomads: Archeologist Finkelstein's model has desert-dwelling Canaanite herders slowly moving west into the hills and taking up farming.

---

[3] The Philistines were a Greek Aegean "Sea People" which defeated the Canaanites in the southern maritime plain and set up city-states with Aegean architectural and cultural features. See Parkes, p. 17 and Peters, pp. 138-139.

[4] Dever, p. 28. But see discussion of Edom below.

[5] Dever, p. 71

[6] Isserlin, p. 58

1.2.3   Israelites as Sedentarizing Canaanite Pastoral Nomads

Finkelstein & Silberman argue that archeologists, taking Joshua at face value, looked in the wrong places – the sites of Canaanite cities, such as Jericho, Bethel, Lachish and Hazor. "While these major tells revealed a great deal about [Canaanite] Late Bronze Age urban culture, they told us next to nothing about the Israelites." These cities were in the coastal plain and valleys, "far from the wooded hill country regions where early Israel emerged." Scholarly indifference and political unrest had made those highlands "an archeological terra incognita." But following the Six Day War, "a young generation of Israeli archeologists, influenced by new trends in world archeology, took to the field with a new method of investigation: their goal was to explore, map, and analyze the ancient landscape of the hill country – rather than only dig."[7]

"These surveys revolutionized the study of early Israel. The discovery of the remains of a dense network of highland villages – all apparently established within the span of a few generations – indicated that a dramatic social transformation had taken place in the central hill country of Canaan around 1200 BCE. There was no sign of violent invasion or even the infiltration of a clearly defined ethnic group. Instead, it seemed to be a revolution in lifestyle. In the formerly sparsely populated highlands from the Judean hills in the south to the hills of Samaria in the north, far from the Canaanite cities that were in the process of collapse and disintegration, about two-hundred fifty hilltop communities suddenly sprang up. Here were the first Israelites."[8]

It's fitting, perhaps even just, that it was young Israeli archeologists, veterans like Yadin before them of war for Israel's survival, who found the first Israelites, if that's what they did. But did they? How do we know they were Israelites? Finkelstein & Silberman:

"Although there is no way to know if ethnic identities had been fully formed at this time, we identify these distinctive highland villages as 'Israelite' since many of them were continuously occupied well into the period of the monarchies – an era from which we have abundant sources, both biblical and extra-biblical, testifying that their inhabitants consciously identified themselves as Israelites."[9]

---

[7] Finkelstein & Silberman, pp. 105-106.
[8] Finkelstein & Silberman, p. 107.
[9] Finkelstein & Silberman, p. 107n. See also Isserlin, *The Israelites*, p. 59: "It is also true that the highland culture being discussed here developed, without any detectable later intrusions, into that of historical Israel."

Who were these highland villagers? Finkelstein & Silberman cite Izbet Sartah, where earliest settlement remains were found intact beneath later ones. They describe it as a continuous oval of buildings surrounding a large open courtyard, suggesting sheep and goat herding, along with grain farming. Similar oval sites have been found in the Bronze and Iron Age Mideast, and in 19th and 20th century Bedouin encampments. "The people living in these sites – both past and present – were pastoralists primarily concerned with protecting their flocks. All this indicates that a large proportion of the first Israelites were once pastoral nomads."[10]

This pastoralists' settlement wave occurred, in this model, with the 12th century BCE collapse of Egyptian rule over Canaan, leaving farmers with no grain surplus to trade. Forced to raise their own grain, desert-fringe pastoralists shifted more and more into agriculture. Eventually a permanent shift to farming occurred.[11]

"The process that we describe here is, in fact, the opposite of what we have in the Bible: the emergence of early Israel was an outcome of the collapse of the Canaanite culture, not its cause. And most of the Israelites did not come from outside Canaan – they emerged from within it. There was no mass Exodus from Egypt. There was no violent conquest of Canaan. Most of the people who formed early Israel were local people – the same people we see in the highlands throughout the Bronze and Iron Ages. The early Israelites were – irony of ironies -- themselves originally Canaanites!"[12]

1.2.4 Israelites as Rebelling Canaanite Peasants

Dever advances an indigenous origins model of Canaanite peasants moving up into the hills. He begins with points on which he, Finkelstein and "most archeologists" agree: the great relevance of the recent Israeli surveys; the occurrence of an Iron I demographic surge in the hill country, which he credits Finkelstein for documenting; and that "the highland settlers were not foreign invaders, but came mostly from somewhere within Canaanite society."[13]

He then lists the "critical points of disagreement," primarily that Finkelstein himself estimates far too few nomads to cause the hills' population jump. "There must have been a very sizable

---

[10] Finkelstein & Silberman, p. 112
[11] Finkelstein & Silberman, pp. 115-118
[12] Finkelstein & Silberman, p 118
[13] Dever, pp. 153-154.

population increment from someplace else, and early on. Indeed, every other archeologist thinks so; no one follows Finkelstein's almost exclusively resedentarized nomads theory."[14] He further denies that the early hill sites were oval ring or desert fringe or that the Israelite pillar-courtyard house was "some desert nostalgia monumentalized in stone and mudbrick." Dever calls it "first and foremost a successful adaptation to farm life … (food processing, stabling, storage below, living spaces above)."[15]

Then citing, like Finkelstein, Late Bronze Age Canaanite culture's collapse, Dever states "it is time to take up the notion of withdrawal" of factions from Canaanite society once again, "but now with much more new supporting archeological evidence, and with different ideas about its motives." "It was not flight from intolerable conditions or necessarily a revolutionary Yahwistic fervor that propelled people toward the frontier, but rather simply a quest for a new society and a new lifestyle. They wanted to start over."[16]

But: "My theory is speculative, of course; and like Mendenhall's and Gottwald's peasants' revolt it has little direct archeological evidence to support it. Nevertheless our current knowledge of the general archeological context of Canaan toward the end of the Late Bronze Age makes this scenario quite realistic."[17]

In the end, Dever must address for his farmers what Finkelstein had to address for his nomads: How do we know they were Israelite? He lists ethnic group criteria: biological self-perpetuation; shared language and values; a "partly independent 'interaction sphere'"; class by itself and others as "distinct from other categories of the same order"; self-identity boundary rules. The hill country culture, "while continuous in general with that of Late Bronze Age Canaan, exhibits enough changes to mark it as something new." But is it Israelite? "These were the *ancestors* [italics original] – the authentic and direct progenitors – of those who later became the biblical Israelites," hence "proto-Israelites."[18] In support of this lineal descent Dever, like Finkelstein and Isserlin, cites

---

[14] Dever, pp. 157-158
[15] Dever, pp. 158-164
[16] Dever, p. 178
[17] Dever, p. 178
[18] Dever, pp. 193-194

6

Iron I to Iron II continuities: undisturbed growth of a long-resident population until becoming "now clearly Israelite," and technological attributes including house form:

"The most striking continuity between Iron I and Iron II is seen in the extensive use of the pillar-courtyard house until the end of the Monarchy, not only in rural areas but also in built-up urban areas. It becomes, in fact, the standard Israelite house; this is an extremely important clue to ethnicity. . . .The form is authentically Israelite, even if not exclusively so. Several younger Israelite archeologists formerly skeptical about the positivist views of their teachers have recently argued that the characteristic, preferred Israelite house, from the beginning of the nation's history to its end, gives us unique insights into 'Israelite' mentality, especially its celebration of the family as the basic unit of society. This is certainly an inheritance from our Iron I proto-Israelite culture."[19]

On recognition as an ethnic group by outsiders, Dever cites as a "compelling – I would say conclusive – piece of evidence justifying the term," the reference to "Israel" on the "Victory" Stele of the Egyptian pharaoh Merneptah, c. 1210 BCE, claiming "Israel is laid waste; his seed is not." Dever says it "tells us the following:"

"1. There existed in Canaan by 1210 B.C. a cultural and probably political entity that called itself 'Israel' and was known to the Egyptians by that name.

"2. This Israel was well enough established by that time among the other peoples of Canaan to have been perceived by Egyptian intelligence as a possible challenge to Egyptian hegemony.

"3. This Israel did not comprise an organized state like others in Canaan, but consisted rather of loosely affiliated peoples – that is, an ethnic group.

"4. This Israel was not located in the lowlands, under Egyptian domination, but in the more remote central hill country, on the frontier."[20]

1.3 The Case for The "Conquest"

1.3.1 A Pea Under the Indigenous Mattress?

Finkelstein's summation – "The early Israelites were – irony of ironies – themselves originally Canaanites" – is hedged:

"The process that we describe here is, in fact, the opposite of what we have in the Bible: the emergence of early Israel was an outcome of the collapse of the Canaanite culture, not its cause. And **most** of the Israelites did not come from outside Canaan – they emerged from within it. There was no **mass** Exodus from Egypt. There was no violent conquest of Ca-

---

[19] Dever, pp. 194-200
[20] Dever, pp. 201-206

7

naan. **Most** of the people who formed early Israel were local people – the same people we see in the highlands throughout the Bronze and Iron Ages. The early Israelites were – irony of ironies -- themselves originally Canaanites!" [21] [emphasis added]

And the farmers model has external origins' strains. Isserlin:

"Mendenhall and Gottwald accepted that a point of crystallization for this process was provided by the religious ideas which a group of followers of Moses brought with them (Gottwald thought they became effective after the social revolution had started). More recent adherents of this view seem little interested in such a factor, and the rise of Israel is for them largely the result of social developments among the Canaanites." [22]

Dever likewise allows for possibly "even perhaps an 'Exodus group'" in his proto-Israelite "motley crew."[23]

Chaim Herzog:

"Recent theories of a completely peaceful takeover do not stand up to comparison with any of the well known acquisitions in antiquity of a national homestead at the expense of the indigenous population. Nor is there any sound explanation for the complementary theory that the Israelites crystallized out of the existing Canaanite population. Here too, we lack, other than certain variously interpreted archeological data, any true historical comparison. To mention only two problems with these theories: how and why did a random group of disowned and resettled farmers (as the forefathers of the Israelites were thought to have been) develop, in their own country and without compulsion, a distinct national entity based on innovatory monotheism – a religion categorically opposed to their deeply rooted ancient beliefs? How could they develop a lore and traditions, wholly based on a nomadic past with a rather strange and, on the face of it, far from ennobling tradition of servitude in Egypt?" [24]

Isserlin, to whom Israel's origins "remain obscure," shook his head and concluded:

"None of the [alternative to conquest] hypotheses outlined above account satisfactorily for the rise of the peculiar local entity which was Israel, nor is there support for them in biblical traditions. The origins of Israel may in fact have been far more complex, involving not only conquest by a limited group with a novel religion, but also some peaceful infiltration, as well as the adhesion of dispossessed elements. Such a combination would not be entirely without parallels." [25]

---

[21] Finkelstein & Silberman, p. 118
[22] Isserlin, p. 58
[23] Dever, p. 182
[24] Herzog & Gichon, p. 40
[25] Isserlin, pp. 58-59

And is, doubtless, at least partly correct.

1.3.2   Joshua vs. Albright & Wright

There's daylight between Albright-Wright and the Bible. Prof. James K. Hoffmeier, author of *"Israel In Egypt: The Evidence for the Authenticity of the Exodus Tradition"* (1996), agrees that the early "Albright-Wright synthesis has been rightly challenged by virtually every recent scholarly investigation concerned with the origins of Israel debate," but adds that "its critics have widely assumed that the 'conquest' theory of Albright-Wright and their followers is one and the same as the 'biblical' description," and that the repudiation of Albright-Wright thereby repudiated Joshua.[26] Hoffmeier argues that Albright-Wright goes far beyond destruction claims in the Bible, and that absent evidence of these beyond-the-Bible claims doesn't militate against the Biblical Conquest:

"Wright includes Megiddo in his list of cities conquered by Israel, and yet nowhere in Joshua or Judges is Megiddo reported to be conquered. The killing of its king (which could have occurred in a battle elsewhere) is recorded in Joshua 12:21, but a coexistence between the Israelites and residents of Megiddo is described in Joshua 17:21 and Judges 1:27."[27]

Hoffmeier asserts: "To 'besiege,' 'assault,' or 'take' a city does not mean it was destroyed." The cities described as "taken" in Joshua 10 were "probably were not destroyed or leveled, thus leaving no detectable [destruction] evidence in the archeological record." But: "The Joshua narratives . . . are very clear when the Israelites did in fact burn a city, which *would* [emphasis original] leave its mark in the archeological record. The book of Joshua reports only three cities destroyed by fire . . .; that is, Jericho Josh. 6:24), Ai (Josh. 8-19-20, 28), and Hazor (Josh. 11:11)."[28]

Jericho, Ai and Hazor

So what about Jericho, Ai and Hazor?

In 1996, archeologist Amnon Ben Tor uncovered what Hoffmeier called "sensational, charred remains of the Late Bronze Age palace," including "the deliberate decapitation and mutilation of statues of deities," consistent with "the charge of Moses to the Israel-

---

[26] Hoffmeier, p. 33
[27] Hoffmeier, p 33
[28] Hoffmeier, pp 34-35

ites," and "with the description of the sack of Hazor in Joshua 11,"[29] but the dating turned out to be too early.

But, Hoffmeier claims, Jericho and Ai pose the main tests.

"Perhaps the most severe blow to the conquest theory has been the archeological problems posed at Jericho and et-Tell, thought to be Ai. Since these are among the most thoroughly documented and celebrated sites of Israelite victories in Joshua (2, 6-8, 29), and since the text is explicit about the cities being burned (Josh. 6:24; 8:28), these sites should serve as test cases for the conquest model and the historicity of the Joshua narratives."[30]

Prof. Garstang of Liverpool University excavated Jericho in the 1930s and dated a c. 1400 BCE "massive destruction and conflagration" to the Israelite conquest, in line with a since-marginalized "early" Exodus. However, in the 1950s the highly respected Dame Kathleen Kenyon excavated Jericho, using more exacting methods and analytical tools, and dated the destruction to the Middle Bronze Age (c. 1550 BCE), a redating accepted by archeologists and biblical scholars alike. "Kenyon also discovered that during the Late Bronze period, when the Israelites were thought to have 'conquered' Jericho, it was scarcely occupied and the levels were badly eroded."[31] So, Hoffmeier acknowledges, "Jericho became a liability to the conquest theory." But in 1990 an archeologist named Bryant G. Wood re-evaluated the Jericho ceramic evidence and argued for restoring Garstang's original Late Bronze dating and attributing the destruction to the Israelites. Hoffmeier acknowledges that Wood's suggestions "have not been received warmly" by archeologists," but argues that Wood's arguments "for redating the ceramics that Kenyon assigned to the Middle Bronze Age to the Late Bronze Age must be considered carefully." For Hoffmeier, "the problem of Jericho has been reopened...."[32]

As for Ai: Albright-Wright had dated et-Tell's "impressive destruction" to the 13th century and Garstang to c. 1400. When later excavations showed a hiatus from 2400 to 1200, Albright and Wright posited what even Hoffmeier calls a "contorted hypothesis" that "Beitin (which they'd excavated earlier) was the site de-

---

[29] Hoffmeier, p 35
[30] Hoffmeier, p 6
[31] Hoffmeier, pp. 6-7
[32] Hoffmeier, pp. 6-7

stroyed by the Israelites, but the tradition was transferred to et-Tell because of the impressive destruction there." "Thus," Hoffmeier concludes, "Ai joined Jericho as a major embarrassment for proponents of the conquest model, and consequently Noth's etiological explanation for the Joshua narratives has enjoyed a resurgence of popularity. Even the normally conservative Yigael Yadin, who in the main defended the conquest theory, conceded the point on Ai: 'we must interpret the Biblical account as etiological.'"[33] But must we? Hoffmeier isn't so sure, noting the inconsistency of scholars who accept Joshua on the location of Ai, which is in issue, while rejecting it on what happened there, "an untendentious, realistic story that does not tax credulity."[34]

Hoffmeier leaves the effect of the Albright-Wright model's repudiation on the Biblical conquest account's historicity with this:

"A careful reading of the text of Joshua suggests a far more modest military outcome than those advanced by twentieth-century biblical scholars either supporting or critiquing the conquest model. So it appears that the real contradiction was between the model and the archeological record, not the record and the narrative of Joshua and Judges. The conquest model has become something of a straw man that ostensibly represented the biblical record, the latter being guilty by association with the former."

Hoffmeier concludes that the idea of a group of tribes coming to Canaan, militarily taking a number of cities and areas over some years, burning just three cities, and coexisting alongside the Canaanites and other ethnic groups for a period of time before the beginnings of monarchy, does not require blind faith. Moreover,

" . . . the idea that the Israelites would have destroyed and leveled cities indiscriminately, makes little sense for they intended to live in this land. A scorched-earth policy is only logical for a conqueror who has no thought of occupying the devastated land. After the battles had been fought and the land divided up among the tribes, Israel is said to have occupied 'a land on which you have not labored, and cities which you had not built, and you dwell therein; you eat the fruit of vineyards and olive yards which you did not plant' (Josh. [sic]24:13). This suggests that the arrival of the Israelites did not significantly affect the cultural continuity of the Late Bronze Age and may explain why there is no evidence of an intrusion into the land from outsiders, for they became heirs of the material culture of the Canaanites." [35]

---

[33] Hoffmeier, p. 7
[34] Hoffmeier, p. 7
[35] Hoffmeier, pp. 42-44

Gibeon

Another familiar Sunday school city is Gibeon, where "Joshua made the sun stand still." If so, there were apparently no Late Bronze Age Canaanite observers to be impressed, per Finkelstein & Silberman's datings of Gibeon ruins as only earlier and later.[36]

"But see," as they taught us in law review days to cite conflicting cases on point but not quite "contra," James B. Pritchard, *Gibeon: Where the Sun Stood Still, The Discovery of the Biblical City* (1962). His excavations found evidence bearing on Late Bronze Age occupation of Gibeon.

"This seeming discrepancy between the biblical record and the actual remains at the site was suddenly resolved in 1960, when we opened two tombs to find in them a rich assortment of Late Bronze Age pottery. That they were no isolated burials of the nomads of the period seems certain from the fact that one of them, Tomb 10B, had the largest number of objects (147 catalogued objects and 73 beads) that we have as yet found in a tomb at el-Jib [identified as ancient Gibeon]. These richly furnished tombs of the Late Bronze period indicate that Gibeon was in existence in the period immediately before the time of Joshua, although we have thus far failed to find the particular area of the mound which the city of that period occupied.

"The importance of this belated discovery of evidence for the Late Bronze occupation at Gibeon is heightened by the archeological situation at the sites of two other cities [Jericho and Ai?] mentioned in the biblical narratives dealing with the conquest of Joshua."[37]

Biblical Edom

The Bible says that at the outset of their Conquest campaign, before crossing the Jordan into the Promised Land, the Israelites encountered the Edomites in southern Transjordan, and were denied passage through Edom. But "we now know," wrote Dever in a passage quoted above, "that occupation of Edom did not begin until much later, and even then it was extremely sparse. And the area remained largely nomadic until perhaps the 7th century B.C., when a sort of semi-sedentary 'tribal state' finally emerged." "What this means is that there cannot have been a king of Edom to have denied the Israelites access, since Edom did not achieve any kind of statehood until the 7th century B.C."[38]

---

[36] Finkelstein & Silberman, pp. 81-83
[37] Pritchard, p. 136
[38] Dever, p.28

Contra: Jerusalem Post (www.jpost.com), Feb. 21, 2005:

"Jordanian Dig Confirms Biblical Edom

"Just-published evidence from a US-directed archeological dig in Jordan further authenticates the Bible's descriptions of the existence of the ancient nation of Edom during the eras of King David and his son, King Solomon. . . .

"The new study . . . contradicts much contemporary scholarship claiming – on the basis of no physical evidence – that no Edomite state existed before the 8th century BCE. Until the new discovery, many scholars said the Bible's numerous references to ancient Israel's interactions with Edom could not be valid.

"While previous investigations in Edom had been carried out in the Jordanian highland zone and put the rise of the Edomite kingdom during the 8th to 6thcenturies BCE, the new archeological data from modern-day Jordan presents strong evidence for the involvement of Edom with neighboring ancient Israel as described in the Bible and indicates the existence of the biblical nation of Edom at least as early as the 10th Century BCE – when David and Solomon were alive."

This was a real Conquest-era Edom. The article cited Edomite lowlands copper production radiocarbon-dated to the 12th-9th centuries BCE, "massive fortifications and industrial-scale metal production activities, as well as over 100 building complexes," and "additional evidence of metal-working activities at the site in the period around 1200 to 900 BCE." The researchers claim they "push back the beginnings of Edom 300 years earlier than the current scholarly consensus and show the presence of complex societies, perhaps a kingdom, much earlier than previously assumed."

1.3.3 Sitz im Leben

Some grant no independent evidentiary weight to the Bible. Melvin Konner began his 2003 book *Unsettled: An Anthropology of The Jews*, that the Bible "will not figure in any sense in this account of how the people of Israel lived, and how they became the Jews – except when there is independent corroborating evidence. With all due respect to believers, I write here as an anthropologist who does not believe anything that is not scientifically proven."[39]

Independent of faith-based belief, what evidentiary weight should we accord the Bible? Konner's rejection of the Bible as evidence "except when there is independent corroborating evidence" sum-

---

[39] Konner, .p. xvii

13

marily deprives non-externally corroborated passages of the evidentiary weight normally accorded ancient documents fitting plausibly into their claimed time and place, told in their literary style and technique, and technically difficult to construct in detail in a later time or distant place. Is the bible, because it's the Bible, entitled to less? We look at biblical battles and Solomon's Temple.

Joshua's Battles

An eminently respectable, far from credulous and naïve,[40] voice on the side of "the Bible as history" was General and President of Israel Chaim Herzog, who with fellow military historian Mordechai Gichon authored a professional analysis of biblical military campaigns, *Battles of the Bible*, originally written in the 1970's but updated and reissued in 2002.

They saw a ring of truth in biblical battle detail, which as military historians they could not dismiss as inventiveness. "Our views as to the intrinsic veracity of the details of the biblical battle reports is sustained by the school of thought that claims for much of the Bible narrative the authenticity of the 'Sitz im Leben,' which means that the matter under discussion truly reflects the social, technological and intellectual background of the period of their composition." They contrasted Homeric description of the Trojan War with the biblical account of Gideon's campaign against the Midianites, observing that in contrast Homer's vagueness,

"the tactical description of the battles of the Bible in their intricate topographical setting and the subsequent detailed and logical interaction between movement, manoeuvres and ground features, shaping the course of the battles, cannot be explained by mere inventiveness. . . . [In Gideon's campaign,] the detailed tactical movements and encounters based on the interaction between specific topographical features and the actions of both friend or foe – over a theatre of war covering some forty miles in length –simply cannot be reproduced anywhere. As every soldier will testify, every battlefield is sui generis in its details.

"We are thus forced to accept the veracity of the tactical narrative of the battles as described in the Bible, although, as mentioned above, occurrences mainly in the pre-monarchal period may have been allocated, by mistake or by intent, to the wrong tribal leader or to the wrong time." [41]

---

[40] Hoffmeier, p. 14: "There has been the tendency for minimalist scholars to think of themselves as strictly objective investigators, the implication being that the historical maximalist is biased, credulous and naïve."

[41] Herzog & Gichon, pp. 22-23

Solomon's Temple

In his 2001 *What Did the Biblical Writers Know and When Did They Know It?*, Dever strongly defended the authenticity of the sitz im leben of Solomon's Temple. Is the Bible's detailed description fantasy, or a plausible account of a 10th century temple?

"Indeed, the 'fabulous' nature of Solomon's temple in the Bible is largely what prompts the revisionists and others to dismiss it as a figment of later writers' and editors' imaginations, fired by the old legends of the 'Golden Age of Solomon.' But is the biblical temple really 'fabulous,' that is, nothing but a fable? Hardly. It might have been so regarded a generation ago; but the fact is that we now have direct Bronze and Iron Age parallels for *every single feature* [emphasis Dever's] of the 'Solomonic temple' as described in the Hebrew Bible; and the best parallels come from, and only from, the Canaanite-Phoenician world of the 15th – 9th centuries." [42]

Dever lists in a chart ten salient features of Solomon's Temple, keyed to biblical references. He then described archeological evidence documenting Solomonic-era authenticity for them.

The special July-October 2009 issue of Biblical Archeology Review (pp. 80-82) includes in its "Ten Top Discoveries" that of the "closest Solomonic parallel" 'Ain Dara Temple in northern Syria, earlier reported in BAR by the site archeologist, John Monson. BAR's 2009 issue: "Nearly every aspect of the 'Ain Dara temple – its age, its size, its plan, its decoration – parallels the vivid description of Solomon's Temple in the Bible." It credited Monson with identifying "more than 30 architectural and decorative" matches.

"It is the date of the 'Ain Dara temple, however, that offers the most compelling evidence for the authenticity of the Biblical account of Solomon's Temple. The 'Ain Dara temple was originally built around 1300 B.C. and remained in use for more than 550 years . . . . As noted by Lawrence Stager of Harvard University, the existence of the 'Ain Dara temple proves that the Biblical description of Solomon's Temple was 'neither an anachronistic account based on later temple archetypes nor a literary creation. The plan, size, date and architectural details fit squarely into the tradition of sacred architecture from north Syria (and probably Phoenicia) from the tenth to the eighth centuries B.C.'"

1.4   Tracing The Jews and Their Book Back To Beginnings

The Hebrew Bible and Jews' religion, traditions and intense feeling for Israel can be traced back astonishingly far into the past.

---

[42] Dever2, p. 145

Continuously for millennia, Jews the world over who cannot speak each others' languages have observed solemn and festive events, starting at sundown on the same night each year according to a calendar, adhered to by no one else in the world, traceable back to Mideast agricultural seasons that had been inscribed on a stone, "the Gezer stone," perhaps as an Israelite schoolboy's lesson, shortly after the time of King David.[43] We'll trace one of those holidays, "*the* holiday," the Jews' peoplehood-defining ceremony back to pre-history. But first we'll trace back the Jews' book, the Hebrew Bible, with strains and sources going back to times perhaps even contemporaneous with many of its recorded events.

1.4.1 JEDP

Everyone who's ever taken an "Old Testament" course remembers learning about the Bible's "J," "E," "D" and "P" sources, to which generations of scholars have painstakingly traced its text.

Dever's 2003 book offers his biblical-strands chronology assessment. First, he states the sources' traditional dating, which has J, the earliest, "dated as early as the 10th century B.C.", E in the 9th, combined as JE in the 8th, D in the 7th, and finally P "sometime during the exilic or post-exilic period (6th century B.C.)." But then he cites the "tendency nowadays" towards closer, later, dating:

"Nowadays, however, there is a tendency to see the Pentateuch (or Tetrateuch) as a more unified work, although dated somewhat later, toward the very end of the Monarchy in the 8th or 7th century B.C. Part of the reason for lowering the date is that archeologists have recently shown that literacy was not widespread in ancient Israel until the 8th century B.C. at the earliest." [44]

But this "tendency" toward later dating, based on archeologists having "recently shown," that "literacy was not widespread in ancient Israel until the 8th century B.C. at the earliest," may have recently taken some hits from findings and analysis evidencing earlier Israelite literacy and earlier, even pre-D, dating of "P":

[1] Tel Zayit

The November 9, 2005, New York Times reported (p. A12):

"In the 10th century B.C., in the hill country south of Jerusalem, a scribe carved his A B C's on a limestone boulder—actually, his aleph-beth-

---

[43] Konner, pp. 11, 23
[44] Dever, pp. 7-8

16

gimel's, for the string of letters appears to be an early rendering of the emergent Hebrew alphabet.

"Archeologists digging in July at the site, Tel Zayit, found the inscribed stone in the wall of an ancient building. After an analysis of the layers of ruins, the discoverers concluded that this was the earliest known specimen of the Hebrew alphabet and important benchmark in the history of writing, they said this week. "The inscription was found in a substantial network of buildings at the site, which led Dr. Tappy [the archeologist directing the dig] to propose that Tel Zayit was probably an important border town established by an expanding Israelite kingdom based in Jerusalem. A border town of such size and culture, Dr. Tappy said, suggested a centralized bureaucracy, political leadership and *literacy levels* that seemed to support the biblical image of the united kingdom of David and Solomon inthe 10th century B.C. . . . ." [emphasis added]

[2] Elah Fortress

Suggesting the substantiality of David's kingdom even more dramatically are findings at another Israelite-Philistine border site, Elah Fortress-Khirbet Qeiyafa, where an ostracon, a broken pottery shard with writing, was unearthed in 2008. "The first Hebrew inscription clearly dated to the tenth century" – Hershel Shanks in BAR, Jan/Feb 2009, p. 43, "it proves that the Hebrews in the earliest years of the United Monarchy were writing," Ibid. The main epigrapher, Dr. Hagai Misgav, contends that this is early Canaanite lettering which remained in use for centuries in this region. Exactly what the ostracon says is still being deciphered, but, says Hebrew University Prof. Yosef Garfinkel, excavator of Elah: ". . . the five-line inscription uncovered at Khirbet Qeiyafa clearly indicates that writing was practiced in this region" in the 10th century BCE. Again, it "tells us for the first time that the people here could read and write at the time of King David, so historical knowledge could be transmitted in writing and not just by oral tradition as some have suggested,' Garfinkle said."

[3] Jerusalem Tomb Amulets:

A BAR 200th issue (July-Oct 2009) article on a Jerusalem tomb by its archeologist, Gabriel Barkey, states that two silver amulets found there, "securely dated" to the late 7th century BCE, contain the Bible's priestly blessing – "words with which observant Jews still bless their children before the Sabbath meal on Friday night" – "generally considered part of P." The article acknowledges (p 126) "major scholarly disagreement" whether P predates the Babylonian exile, and asserts that the amulets' texts "seem to support

17

those who contend that the Priestly Code was already in existence, at least in rudimentary form, in the First Temple period."

[4] Scholar Richard Elliott Friedman's Dating of J, E, P and D

Dever's dating acknowledges earlier written and oral sources:

"Most scholars, however, will also argue as do I that the biblical tradition rests not only on contemporary and earlier documentary sources now lost to us, but also on even earlier oral traditions." [45]

In *The Bible With Sources Revealed*, scholar Richard Elliott Friedman dates J to Judah, and E to Israel, during the divided monarchies, 922 – 722 BCE; their consolidation into JE in Judah after Israel's fall; P to "the Jerusalem priesthood as an alternative to the history told in JE" that was "composed not long after J and E were combined" (rejecting the view of 6th-5th century dating of P); and D to King Josiah's time, with exilic supplementation. [46]

1.4.2 Pesach, Matza and Moror

Scholar Hayyim Schauss traced the Jews' peoplehood-defining ceremony – Pesach, Passover – back to pre-history in *The Jewish Festivals: From Their Beginnings To Our Own Day*, published in English in 1938 as a translation of his original Yiddish work. [47]

". . . Pesach is the oldest of Jewish festivals. Jews observed it in the most ancient of times, in the days when they were still nomadic shepherds in the wilderness. . . ."

". . . a holiday is always older than the interpretation which is given to it. First comes the custom, the ceremony, the observance; no interpretation for them is needed or sought. The ceremony explains itself. Later, after a long time passes, need is found for an interpretation and its rites. So, Pesach was originally a nature festival, an observance of the coming of spring. Later, as time went on, it became a historic and national holiday, the festival of the deliverance from Egypt, and it thus assumed a newer and higher meaning." [48]

Schauss wrote that Pesach is a spring antedating the exodus from Egypt. He cited Moses seeking Pharaoh's permission for them to go out into the wilderness "that they might observe their feast in honor of God," a cause-effect relationship with the Exodus later

---

[45] Dever, p. 8

[46] Friedman, pp. 8-9

[47] See also *Ancient Israel: Its Life and Institutions*, Roland De Vaux, chapter 17, well written and in great detail.

[48] Schauss, p. 39

18

reversed. Pesach's most ancient ceremonies, similar to customs of other ancient peoples, are eerily familiar:

"In the month when the kids and lambs were born, the month that ushered in spring, they observed a festival at full moon (the fourteenth or fifteenth day of the month). Every member of the family took part in the observance of this festival, which was featured by the sacrifice of a sheep or goat from the flock. The sacrifice occurred just before nightfall, after which the animal was roasted whole and all members of the family made a hasty meal in the middle of the night. It was forbidden to break any of the bones of the sacrificial animal or to leave uneaten any part of it by the time daybreak came. One of the chief ceremonies attendant upon the festival was the daubing of the tent-posts with the blood of the slain animal [to ward off misfortune]." [49]

In the land, Pesach was observed more in shepherd-dwelling Judah than Israel, which was more suited for farming. But those who tilled the soil observed "The Festival of Matsos (Unleavened Bread)," which began with the cutting of barley and ended seven weeks later with the reaping of wheat. Again, the ancient practices strike eerily familiar chords in today's Jewish homes:

"Before the start of the barley harvest, the Jews would get rid of all the 'sourdough' (fermented dough used instead of yeast to leaven bread) and the old bread they possessed; everything, in fact, connected with 'chomets,' the leaven of the last year's crop. We cannot know for certain, by now, what was the origin of the removing of all sour dough and the eating of unleavened bread. It was probably regarded as a safeguard against an unproductive year. In later years the Jews created a new interpretation for this old custom, just as they evolved a new meaning for the Pesach eve ceremonies." [50]

Passover, as we know it, is an amalgam of two Israelite festivals:

"We must thus bear in mind that Pesach and the Feast of Unleavened Bread were originally two distinct festivals, observed at the same time. Pesach was the older holiday, the one the Jews brought with them from the desert; the Feast of Unleavened Bread was newer, instituted only after the Jews had settled in Palestine and become farmers. Both were spring festivals, but the Feast of Unleavened Bread was observed by the entire community gathered in a holy place, while Pesach was celebrated in the home as a family festival." [51]

Over time, the Jews forgot the original meanings of Pesach and the Feast of Unleavened Bread. A spring holiday with an historic

---

[49] Schauss, pp. 39-40
[50] Schauss, p. 41
[51] Schauss, p. 43

19

background became more appealing, and so "they began to emphasize Pesach as the festival of the deliverance from Egypt."

"This transition came very easily. The memory of the exodus from Egypt burned brightly in the minds of the Jews, and with it the memory that it was in the first spring month of the year that they had left the land of the Pharaohs. The reliving of that great event in the dawn of Jewish history became the chief motive for the celebration of the spring festival. Spring, the time of liberation for nature, and the idea of human freedom seemed to fit very well together; in this way Pesach became the festival of the freedom of the Jewish people, its deliverance from slavery, and its awakening to a new life."[52]

The customs and symbols were reinterpreted as associated with the deliverance from Egypt. "Passover" came to mean that "God passed over the Jewish homes when he slew the first-born of Egypt." The bread was unleavened because the Israelites had no time to bake it properly in their haste to exit from Egypt. The "bitter herbs" came to symbolize the bitterness of their oppression in Egypt. The "charoses" became a symbol of the mortar mixed by the Jews in building the store-cities of Pharaoh. "'And it shall be when thy son asketh thee in time to come, saying, "What is this?" that thou shalt say unto him: 'By strength of hand the Lord brought us out from Egypt, from the house of bondage.'"

Late Second Temple times saw Passover reach its zenith as a national holiday. Roman-oppressed "Jewish hearts beat faster on the eve of Pesach," in hopes of a second redemption. But Roman customs seeped into observance "in a richer, more luxurious fashion," with wine, soft sofas, and not in haste. Jerusalem Jews offered the sacrifice at the Temple, then took it home to be roasted and eaten by groups, "with ceremonies that are almost identical with the Seder observed by Jews today.[53]

1.5   The Israelites of the Late Bronze/Iron I Age Transition

Whether by Exodus-Conquest or indigenous origin, the Israelites became established in the land by the 12th century BCE, commencing a tenacious homeland attachment of a people to a place which the Jews have maintained with fiercely burning intensity for longer than three thousand years.

---

[52] Schauss, pp. 43-44
[53] Schauss, pp. 46-47

20

Chapter 2

The Jews' Biblical Kingdoms of Israel and Judah

2.1   Pre-Monarchical Israel

2.1.1   Expansion of the Early Hill Country Settlements

From the central hill country, the Israelites spread north into Galilee and south into Judah. Initially, they had no coherent territory. "Judah was isolated from its brethren to the north until David conquered Jerusalem." Canaanite enclaves remained and the lowlands were non-Israelite. Amalekites held the Negev. Israelite tribal groups moved, smaller groups merged into larger, outsiders were taken in. "The ideal community of the Twelve Tribes is, it seems, based on the combination of traditions from various stages of development, and tribal borders probably did not become firmly established much before the coming of the Monarchy."[1] Aegean "sea-people" Philistines settled in the coastal plain c. 1174.[2] But our knowledge of the Israelites remains vague during the Judges, the monarchy under Saul, and even under David and Solomon.

2.1.2   The Period of the Judges

Many modern scholars date the Judges period from the late 13th to mid 11th centuries, briefer than the biblical chronology. Isserlin

---

[1] Isserlin, p. 64
[2] Isserlin, p. 56

wrote that archeology has to some extent confirmed the biblical picture of a rural Israelite society among contemporary Canaanites. There were "local sanctuaries," but that there was "a sacred confederation around the central sanctuary at Shiloh . . . has lost credit." "Major judges . . . like Ehud, Deborah, Gideon, Jephthah and Samson, following a divine call, delivered a greater or smaller part of Israel from oppression by a remarkable variety of outsiders," but "kingship on the Canaanite model" promised more efficient defense and order at home. Following Philistine capture of the ark and likely burning of the Shiloh sanctuary, "tribal separatism" and "theological scruples" gave way to need for a king.[3]

2.2   The United Monarchy

2.2.1   Saul

"Of Saul's reign we know disappointingly little – even its length is disputed, though it must have fallen late in the eleventh century." His tribe, Benjamin, was his mainstay. "Militarily effective for a time," he cleared the Philistines from the central uplands. "Saul failed disastrously, however, to maintain friendly ties with the influential religious establishment, in spite of his zeal for the Lord." Disqualified by Samuel, the last great judge, and given to bouts of depression, he finally tragically succumbed, along with most of his sons, in the lost battle against the Philistines at Mount Gilboa.[4]

2.2.2   David and Solomon

Isserlin credits David with three key events: transfer of power from north to south and establishment of a new dynasty; effective joining of Judah to the main Israelite body in the north; and establishment of a true monarchy. "Jerusalem, which he acquired and made his capital, was his own special possession which provided neutral ground linked previously with neither Israel nor Judah." Here he built a palace, installed a central administration and made Jerusalem the religious centre of Israel by transferring the Ark into a tent-shrine on Mount Moriah, and may have thought of building a temple to house it. "Though David had obtained the kingship of Judah and Israel by offer and compact, religious support added a different dimension, namely that of kingship by divine grace, with

---

[3] Isserlin, pp. 67-68
[4] Isserlin, pp. 68-69

22

the promise that this would be vested in his descendants for ever."[5]
Isserlin here took David as real. But was there King David?

"In spite of the account of David's life and exploits recorded in the Bible, some critics doubt that King David actually existed. As one of them candidly admits, 'I am not the only scholar who suspects that the figure of King David is about as historical as King Arthur' (Philip R. Davies, Biblical Archeology Review, July-August, 1994, p. 55.)"[6]

Finkelstein & Silberman, under the heading "Did David and Solomon Exist?", dismissed biblical portrayal of a "glorious Golden Age," but held that recent discovery of a foreign king's monument and re-interpretation of another's decisively show their Kingdom existed, shifting the issue to its extent and grandeur.

The argument for viewing David as "a mere tribal chieftain of a dusty hill village" was absence of 10th century remains in Jerusalem, also applicable to earlier Late Bronze Age Jerusalem, described in the Egyptian-Canaanite Amarna letters as "a large thriving city." A Jan/Feb 2009 BAR article cited that era's remains as so sparse "some scholars doubted the identification of the Urusalem mentioned in the Amarna documents with the city of Jerusalem" (p 54). The author stated that the site's bedrock is very high, so "only a few poor remnants survived from the Canaanite city that stood there during the Late Bronze Age" (p. 54). He added (p 70), this "is equally true for the period of the United Monarchy," for which we lack corrective documentary evidence. However, the past few years have seen increasingly unearthed evidence pointing to a substantial Davidic era Jerusalem.

[1] The "House of David" Inscription

First came an explosive[7] mid-1990's discovery. Finkelstein:

". . . in the summer of 1993, at the biblical site of Tel Dan in northern Israel, a fragmentary artifact was discovered that would change forever the

---

[5] Isserlin, p. 70

[6] Mario Seiglie, "King David: Man or Myth?" in "The Good News," July/August 1996, United Church of God, www.ucgstp.org/lit/gn/gn005/gn005f02/htm

[7] "In the world of modern Biblical archeology, few discoveries have attracted as much attention as the Tel Dan stela – the ninth century B.C. inscription that furnished the first historical evidence of King David outside the Bible." Biblical Archeology Review, March/April 1994, reprised July/October 2009, p. 82. ". . . by now the reading 'House of David' has been well-nigh universally accepted," id., p. 106.

nature of the debate. It was the 'House of David' inscription, part of a black basalt monument, found broken and reused in a later stratum as a building stone. Written in Aramaic, the language of the Aramean kingdoms of Syria, it related the details of an invasion of Israel by an Aramean king whose name is not mentioned on the fragments that have so far been discovered. But there is hardly a question that it tells the story of the assault of Hazael, king of Damascus, on the northern kingdom of Israel around 835 BCE. This war took place in the era when Israel and Judah were separate kingdoms, and the outcome was a bitter defeat for both.

"The most important part of the inscription is Hazael's boasting description of his enemies:

'[I killed Jeho]ram son of [Ahab] king of Israel, and [I] killed [Ahaz]iahu son of [Jehoram kin]g of *the House of David*. And I set [their towns into ruins and turned] their land into [desolation].'

"This is dramatic evidence of the fame of the Davidic dynasty less than a hundred years after the reign of David's son Solomon. The fact that Judah (or perhaps its capital, Jerusalem) is referred to with only a mention of its ruling house is clear evidence that the reputation of David was not a literary invention of a much later period." [emphasis added]

Finkelstein then cited reinterpretation of the Moabite stone:

"Furthermore, the French scholar Andre Lemaire has recently suggested that a similar reference to the house of David can be found on the famous inscription of Mesha, king of Moab, in the ninth century BCE, which had been found in the nineteenth century east of the Dead Sea. Thus, the house of David was known throughout the region; this clearly validates the biblical description of a figure named David becoming the founder of the dynasty of Judahite kings in Jerusalem.

"The question we must therefore face is no longer one of David and Solomon's mere existence...." [8]

The Bible-skeptic Konner as well found a rock on which to build a biblical kingdom:

"But at a certain point, perhaps eight or nine centuries before the common era, a unified culture composed a unified story: the kingdom of Israel; the House of David. This monarchy, David's line, comes into history's notice perhaps two centuries after the reign of David's son Solomon. It is in the form of a stone tablet inscribed with the words 'House of David.' That is all, but it is substantial. It tells us that by the eighth century before the common era there was a line of kings in Jerusalem descended from David. To many historians, including non-religious ones, it fits with other evidence that a great tribal chieftain and gifted warrior unified the cultures that shared the monotheistic ideal, creating the first Jewish kingdom." [9]

[8] Finkelstein & Silberman, pp. 128.130, 177
[9] Konner, p. 15

Note the words of Konner of the Finkelstein school: "It tells us that by the 8th century before the common era there was a line of kings in Jerusalem descended from David . . . a great tribal chieftain and gifted warrior," not that David himself had been "king."

Outside Jerusalem, there are the "six-chambered gate" northern cities of Megiddo, Gezer and Hazor. 1 Kings 9:15 attributed these cities' rebuilding to Solomon, as did Yadin in dramatic diggings including a validated prediction. Finkelstein attributes them to the time of the divided kingdoms,[10] but the controversy goes on.

[2] King David's Palace?

In 2003, Finkelstein assessed Jerusalem implications for David.

"Jerusalem has been excavated time and again – and with a particularly intense period of investigation of Bronze and Iron Age remains in the 1970s and 1980s under the direction of Yigal Shiloh, of the Hebrew University, at the city of David, the original urban core of Jerusalem. Surprisingly, as Tel Aviv University archeologist David Ussishkin pointed out, fieldwork there and in other parts of biblical Jerusalem failed to provide significant evidence for a tenth century occupation. Not only was any sign of monumental architecture missing, but so were even simple pottery sherds. The types that are so characteristic of the tenth century at other sites are rare in Jerusalem. Some scholars have argued that later, massive building activities in Jerusalem wiped out all signs of the earlier city. Yet excavations in the city of David revealed impressive finds from the Middle Bronze Age and from later centuries of the Iron Age – just not from the tenth century BCE. The most optimistic assessment of this negative evidence is that tenth century Jerusalem was rather limited in extent, perhaps not more than a typical hill country village."[11]

The 8/5/05 *NY Times* ran an article, "King David's Palace: Is This It?", on discovery in Jerusalem's City of David by archeologist Eilat Mazar, grand-daughter of a famed Israeli archeologist, of "a major public building from around the 10th century BC with pottery sherds that date from the time of David and Solomon." She believes it "may be the fabled palace of the biblical King David." The Times assessed: "If she's right, her discovery will be a new salvo in a major dispute in biblical archeology – whether or not the kingdom of David and Samuel [sic, Solomon] was of historical importance," noting "some question whether they were more like small tribal chieftains, reigning over another dusty hilltop."

---

[10] See Finkelstein & Silberman, pp. 135-142
[11] Finkelstein & Silberman, p. 133

The Times stated that "other Israeli archeologists are not so sure that Mazar has found the palace," other suggestions being the Fortress of Zion that David conquered from the Jebusites or other structure on which the Bible is silent. It concluded: "But Mazar's colleagues know that she has found something extraordinary – the partial foundations of a sizable public building, constructed in the Phoenician style,[12] dating from the 10th-9th centuries BC, the time of the united kingdom of David and Solomon." It's not something typical of "another dusty hilltop" or "typical hill country village."

Further details are in the 8/13/05 *Jerusalem Post* article "Shards of Evidence." It states that Mazar found that "what lay immediately underneath the boulders were not ruined city walls, as had been previously thought, but rather the ruins of an immense 3,000-year-old stone building which was surprisingly well-preserved." Here's Mazar's initial account of her findings in the *Jerusalem Post*:

"... it is the piles of pottery found in and around the building that is of the most critical importance to archeologists, since it is through the pottery that the building can be dated. The pottery found under the building dated back to the last phase of the Iron Age I, 12th-11th century BC, just before David conquered Jerusalem, and predates the construction of the building.

"In one of the rooms, Mazar's team also found pottery from Iron Age II of the 10th-9th century BC, leading her to conclude that the building was in use at the time, roughly the period of David's reign in Jerusalem.

"Mazar's team did not find any construction predating the 11th century BC at the site, leading her to exclude the possibility that the building served as a Jebusite citadel, such as the Fortress of Zion that David captured from the Jebusites, as recounted in Samuel II 5:7. 'It is unrealistic to assume that the Fortress of Zion was built in the very last days before King David captured the city,' she said."

The New York Times article includes Mazar's reference to a last conversation she'd had with her famous grandfather, archeologist

---

[12] Re the Times' recognition that Mazar's find is "a sizeable public building, constructed in the Phoenician style" see Rachel Ginsberg, Reclaiming Biblical Jerusalem, aish.com/jw/j/48961251.html: "According to the Bible, David's palace was constructed by Hiram, King of Tyre, the contemporary Phoenician ruler and his ally against the Philistines. Mazar, an expert in Phoenician construction from her excavations at Achziv on Israel's northern coast, attests that this building bears the mark of Phoenician construction, not likely to be found otherwise in the Judean hills."

Benjamin Mazar, who'd encouraged her to follow up the work of Kathleen Kenyon, who'd found at the City of David site "well-worked stones and proto-aeolic capitals, which decorated the tops of columns, evidence of a large, decorative building."

The debate whether what Mazar unearthed is King David's palace continues. Editor Hershel Shanks, in his First Person column in the March/April 2009 issue of BAR (p. 4): "Although Mazar recognizes that the identification with David is not certain, she has no better suggestion. And neither does anybody else."

[3] Tel Zayit

In chapter 1's quote of the Tel Zayit archeologist's assessment of what the 10th century abecedary uncovered there shows, I italicized his words "literacy levels" as bearing on when the Hebrew Bible could have been committed to writing. Here's that quotation again, with different words emphasized:

"A border town of such size and culture, Dr. Tappy said, suggested *a centralized bureaucracy, political leadership* and literacy levels *that seemed to support the biblical image of the united kingdom of David and Solomon in the 10th century B.C. . . . .*" [emphasis added]

In 2008, Profs. Tappy and McCarter edited a collection of contributions, *Literate Culture and Tenth-Century Canaan: The Tel Zayit Abecedary in Context*. In his contribution, Prof. Tappy concluded (p. 37) that Tel Zayit "helped to open Judah's southwestern frontier already by the mid-10th century B.C.E. Its very existence in this area made an important symbolic statement for the cultural core that lay in the highlands to the east." In his own Johns Hopkins' University Gazette (July 13, 2009) article, McCarter stated that the archeology of Tel Zayit shows that in the 10th century the site was linked culturally with the highlands to the east, not the coastal plain to the west, so that it was probably controlled by Jerusalem, and that, seen in this light, the discovery of the Tel Zayit inscription is strong evidence for the traditional view of a substantial Jerusalem-based 10th century BCE Israelite kingdom.

[4] Elah Fortress-Khirbet Qeiyafa

That second King David-era Judah-Philistine border site, Elah Fortress, exploded into public view in an Oct. 30, 2008, NYT article, closely followed by AP, CNN and many other reports. The Israeli education-through-archeology organization Foundation

27

Stone[13] developed public information on the impacts of a succession of three electrifying discoveries at Elah in what BAR editor Hershel Shanks called the best archeological publicity in 50 years.

[1] The first astounding discovery was the sheer massiveness of this early 10th or late 11th century[14] BCE border fortress. The AP quoted the site archeologist, Hebrew University's Yigael Yadin Chair of Archeology Yosef Garfinkel, that the massive 200,000-ton stone fortress indicates "that a powerful Israelite kingdom existed at the time of the Old Testament's King David." The *New York Times* quoted him: "This was the main road to Jerusalem, the strategic site to protect the kingdom of Jerusalem. If they built a fortification here, it was a real kingdom, pointing to urban cities and a centralized authority in Judah in the 10th century BCE."

The 11/3/08 *National Geographic News* said that it is not settled whether the fortress was Israelite or Philistine, but quoted Garfinkel that "pottery at the fortress is similar to that found at other Israelite sites, and that there are no pig remains – an indicator that often distinguishes Israelite from Philistine sites." At an archeologists' conference, Prof. Garfinkel listed nine reasons supporting classification of Elah Fortress as Israelite.[15] But what if it

---

[13] I had earlier met Foundation Stone's co-Director, Rabbi Barnea Levi Selavan. We've remained in contact, and much of the information about Elah Fortress here derives from my communications with him.

[14] The dating was based on pottery typology confirmed by dozens of experts and later by Oxford University dating of burnt olive pits, found in the clear destruction layer context. The range of dates is approximately 970 BCE to 1050 BCE, clearly before the Egyptian Shishak of the Bible, Sheshonq I's, invasion of Israel, assumed to be in 925 BCE.
Thus, the city is at least from the time of David and Solomon, and maybe earlier; even from Saul's time.

[15] In a PDF file containing ASOR 2008 Conference abstracts, Prof. Garfinkel lists nine reasons for "Why the city [Elah Fortress-Sha-arayim] is Judean": "A. General Arguments: 1. Geographical location in Judah; 2. Sha'arayim: mentioned in Judah's city list [the name means 'two gates']; 3. Fortified field cities are known only in Judah; 4. Casemate city walls are known only in Judah; 5. Main entrance facing Judah; B. Material Culture: 6. No pig bones; 7. Aren Maier of Bar Ilan University: Gath pottery is different; 8. Petrographic analysis: local Elah valley pottery; 9. Hebrew inscription.." Also, at an informal gathering of scientists were excavators of Gath, Ekron, Tel Batash-Timna, Ashkelon and other Philistine cities, who said with one voice that "this is not a coastal assemblage" – Sy Gittin of the Albright Institute, excavator of Tel

isn't? Even if it is Philistine, which Garfinkel firmly denies, Rabbi Selavan quotes him in a 10/20/08 Biblical Studies article, "even so it shows here an opposing force of might."

[2] The second electrifying discovery at Elah was the ostracon, mentioned in chapter 1, the 15 sq. cm pottery shard identified as "the first Hebrew inscription clearly dated to the tenth century" – Hershel Shanks in BAR, Jan/Feb 2009, p. 43. "It proves that the Hebrews in the earliest years of the United Monarchy were writing," Ibid. Some of the words were "king," "judge," – verb or noun – and "slave." Because of the conjunction "al ta'as – do not do!", epigrapher Dr. Hagai Misgav concluded the text was ancient Hebrew. While the writing's content is under discussion, it shows that at least the elite communicated in writing 3000 years ago, in the same language as the Bible, and hence bears on the substantiality of the 10th century BCE Jerusalem-based kingdom.

[3] It was still not clear which city this might be. Elah Fortress lies in the heart of the cities identified as Sochoh and Azeka, and Yarmut and Adulam, in the region identified with the battle of David and Goliath in Samuel 1:17, and in the geographic area of Judah's tribal inheritance mentioned in Joshua 15:35. Yet, at this stage, some scholars, such as Nadav Neeman, still claimed it was a Philistine city. One consideration was the exposed city gate faces west, with paths leading straight into Philistine territory, passing Gath, about 10 km away. The towers of Ashdod on the coast are visible standing in the gate. The city gate always faces the safe side for the residents, so this by itself was a reasonable claim, ignoring the pottery topology, petrography, and other factors.

Then came the third discovery, that of the unique, extraordinarily massive second gate. A JTA article on Nov, 16, 2008, quoted archeologist Garfinkel's electrifying announcement of "a newly discovered second gate" at Elah. YNet on Nov, 20 quoted Garfinkel as having the second gate, "the only one of its kind found in the

---

Miqne-Ekron. The petrography, the chemical makeup of the pottery executed by David Ben Shimon of the Hebrew University showed it was local ware from the valley area. The Tel Aviv University excavators of Judean Bet Shemesh said the pottery matched their early Iron Age II pottery style, as reported to me by Rabbi Selavan.

Kingdoms of Judah or Israel to date," as "revealing the Biblical name of the city: Sha'arayim' – literally meaning two gates."

This two-gate city is mentioned in Joshua and in the story of the Philistines' flight after Goliath's death, as their bodies littered the path of Sha'arayim until Gath and Ekron. No other biblical city has been found with two gates. This second gate faces Judah, and is the most massive gate ever found in the country! Each stone flanking the gate weighs at least 10 tons. So the southeast entrance facing Judah was the main gate, while the western gate, convenient in times of peace for trade with the coast, was still powerfully fortified in case of war. The eastern gate, exposed down to bedrock, has at least four chambers like the western gate.

But it is the Elah dig's archeologist, Prof. Garfinkel, who drives home most vividly the meaning of his Elah excavations for David:

"What is the historical value of the biblical narrative concerning the period of the United Monarchy? In the early days of research it was accepted as an accurate historical account [citing B. Mazar and Yadin]. Since the 1980's serious doubts have been raised regarding this tradition, suggesting that it is merely a literary compilation dating from centuries later [citing Thompson and Davies]. King David was, according to this view, a purely mythological figure. Although the inscription on the Tel Dan stele clearly indicates that he was indeed a historical figure [citing Biran and Naveh], it is unclear if he was the ruler of a large empire or a small, dusty 'cow town.'

"The geopolitical circumstances in the Elah Valley during the late 11th – early10th centuries are quite clear. . . ."

Citing Bible references to Israelite-Philistine conflict and carbon-dating of Elah to David's time, Garfinkel says:

"The front side of the [second-to-be-discovered, Jerusalem-facing] gate is composed of two monumental blocks of stone, one on each side. Each stone has an estimated weight of 10 tons. This is the most massive gate ever found in any biblical city to date. The enormous efforts invested in the gate's construction far exceed technical requirements and was clearly intended as a statement of power and authority.

"The biblical text, the single-phase city at Khirbet Qeiyafa, and the radio metric dates each stands alone as significant evidence clearly indicating that the biblical tradition does bear authentic geographical memories from the 10thcentury BCE Elah Valley. There is no ground for the assumption that these traditions were fabricated in the late 7th century or in the Hellenistic period."[16]

---

[16] Garfinkel & Ganor, The Journal of Hebrew Scriptures, vol. 8, art. 22.

[5] King Solomon's Jerusalem Wall?

On February 26, 2010, *National Geographic News* reported:

"A 3,000 year-old defensive wall possibly built by King Solomon has been unearthed in Jerusalem, according to the Israeli archeologist [Eilat Mazar] who led the excavation. The discovery appears to validate a Bible passage, she says."

The article reported that the wall stands along the 10th century BCE edge of Jerusalem, between the Temple Mount and City of David, and was part of a defensive complex with buildings and tower. Artifacts at the site, characteristic of the second half of the 10th century, set the date to Solomon's time, says Mazar. Hebrew inscriptions bearing impressions "to the king" and Hebrew names were found on storage vessels. It quoted Mazar that the discovery is "the first archeological evidence" of the structure mentioned in Kings I as a defensive wall built by Solomon, and cites Finkelstein as agreeing that it's possible King Solomon constructed the wall."

2.3   The Kingdoms of Israel and Judah

2.3.1   The Northern Kingdom of Israel

Finkelstein & Silberman contend that though Israel and Judah had much uniquely in common – worship of YHWH (among other deities), shared heroes, legends and tales of a common ancient past, and their shared Hebrew language and eventually script –, the two biblical kingdoms were "very different from each other in their demographic composition, economic potential, material culture, and relationship with their neighbors." [17] We'll revisit this after tracing the northern kingdom's career. Finkelstein & Silberman make much of the differences, questioning the "Israeliteness" of Israel. We'll take issue with that, arguing that their own words show deeper "Israeliteness" of Israel than they seem to accept.

On the northern kingdom itself, Finkelstein & Silberman wrote in *The Bible Unearthed* that the biblical picture of a glorious Jerusalem-based united kingdom, followed by dual kingdoms only one of which, Judah, was virtuous, was painted in Judah after Israel's fall, but that actually the biblically-slighted northern kingdom of Israel was the larger and more powerful of the two.

---

[17] Finkelstein & Silberman, p. 159

Three foreign rulers' inscriptions shed extra-biblical light on the northern kingdom during the Omride dynasty – Omri (884-873), Ahab (873-852), Ahaziah (852-851) and Jehoram (851-842).[18]

[1] The Mesha stele, "the first non-biblical description of the Omrides ever found" [and recently reinterpreted as referencing the "House of David" as well], relates how that 9th-century BCE Moabite king, mentioned in 2 Kings 3 as a rebellious vassal of Israel, had recovered territory from Israel kings Omri and Ahab, in the process confirming that "the kingdom of Israel reached far east and south of its earlier heartland in the central hill country."[19]

[2] The second extra-biblical reference to Israel (also the most-acknowledged reference to Judah as the "House of David") is the c. 835 BCE inscription of the Aram-Damascus king Hazael, mentioned several times in the Bible, at Dan. Again, the foreign king's boasts of recovering lands help establish the former extent of Israel's sway. "The kingdom of Israel under the Omrides stretched from the vicinity of Damascus throughout the central highlands and valleys of Israel, all the way to the southern territory of Moab, ruling over considerable populations of non-Israelites."[20]

[3] Third, there is "dramatic evidence" of Israel's military might on a dark stone monument known as the Monolith Inscription by Assyrian king Shalmaneser III, who ruled 858-824 BCE, found at an Assyrian site in the 1840's, recording the forces of an alliance 'unsuccessfully' arrayed against him, including "2,000 chariots, 10,000 foot soldiers of Ahab, the Israelite." Finkelstein & Silberman: "Not only is this the earliest non-biblical evidence of a king of Israel, it is clear from the mention of the 'heavy arms' (chariots) that Ahab was the strongest member of the anti-Assyrian coalition. And although the great Shalmaneser claimed victory, the practical outcome of this confrontation spoke much louder than royal boasts. Shalmaneser quickly returned to Assyria, and at least for a while the Assyrian march to the west was blocked."[21]

"Thus we learn from three ancient inscriptions (ironically from three of Israel's bitterest enemies) information that dramatically supplements the

---

[18] Omride dates taken from Finkelstein & Silberman, p. 171
[19] Finkelstein & Silberman, p. 177
[20] Finkelstein & Silberman, pp. 177-178
[21] Finkelstein & Silberman, p. 178

biblical account. . . . Omri and his successors were in fact powerful kings who expanded the territory of their kingdom and maintained what was certainly one of the largest standing armies in the region. And they were deeply involved in international power politics (at a time when the kingdom of Judah was passed over in silence in Shalmaneser's inscription) in a continuing effort to maintain their independence against regional rivals and the looming threat of the Assyrian Empire." [22]

Despite what Finkelstein & Silberman call "sketchy" description of Israel in the Bible – "Except for the mention of elaborate palaces in Samaria and Jezreel – there is almost no reference to the size, scale, and opulence of their realm"[23] – "the house of Omri," as the Assyrian sources themselves called it, was quite substantial.

Enormous site engineering was done at the Omride capital, Samaria: "massive earth-moving operations," an "enormous wall" of linked rooms "framing the summit and the upper slopes in a large rectangular enclosure" filled with "thousands of tons of earth hauled from the vicinity . . . in some places almost twenty feet deep." "A royal acropolis of five acres was thus created." With what to compare it? "This huge stone and earth construction can be compared in audacity and extravagance (though perhaps not in size) only to the work that Herod the Great carried out almost a millennium later on the Temple Mount in Jerusalem."[24]

Finkelstein & Silberman cite Samaria as "only the beginning of the discovery of Omride grandeur." Astonishingly impressive Omride construction, and redatings from Solomonic to Omride times Megiddo, Hazor, Dan and elsewhere,[25] force this conclusion:

"Archeologically and historically, the redating these cities from Solomon's era to the time of the Omrides has enormous implications. It removes the only archeological evidence that there ever was a united monarchy based in Jerusalem and suggests that David and Solomon were, in political terms, little more than hill country chieftains, whose administrative reach remained on a fairly local level, restricted to the hill country. [This predates the discoveries of 'David's palace' and Elah.] More important, it shows that despite the biblical emphasis on the uniqueness of Israel, a highland kingdom of a thoroughly conventional Near Eastern type arose in the north in the early ninth century BCE. [26]

---

[22] Finkelstein & Silberman, pp. 179-180
[23] Finkelstein & Silberman, p 180
[24] Finkelstein & Silberman, pp. 179-180
[25] Finkelstein & Silberman, pp. 183-186
[26] Finkelstein & Silberman, pp. 189-190

They went on (pp 191-194) to cite evidence that this Omride "highland kingdom of a thoroughly conventional Near Eastern type" had a large non-Israelite Canaanite element which made its influence felt, including through Late Bronze Age "cultural continuity." From this, they drew a second dramatic conclusion:

"That is why it is difficult to insist, from a strictly archeological perspective, that the kingdom of Israel as a whole **was ever particularly Israelite** in either the ethnic, cultural, or religious connotations of that name as we understand it from the perspective of the later biblical writers. The Israeliteness of the northern kingdom was in many ways a late monarchic Judahite idea." [27] [emphasis added]

So what arguments can we muster that this last-quoted Finkelstein & Silberman conclusion – that it's difficult to insist from the archeological record that Israel "was ever particularly Israelite" – is inconsistent with what they also wrote in *The Bible Unearthed*?

[1] Israel and Judah had *much unique* "Israeliteness" in common: Finkelstein & Silberman wrote on page 159 of their book:

"There is **no doubt** that the two Iron Age states – Israel and Judah – had **much in common**. Both [uniquely] worshiped YHWH (among other deities). Their peoples [uniquely] shared many legends, heroes, and tales about a common, ancient past. They also spoke similar languages, or dialects of Hebrew [uniquely], and by the eighth century BCE, both wrote [uniquely] in the same script." [emphasis added]

[2] Israel was consciously a dual-ethnicities kingdom, not a melting of Israelites into Canaanite culture: The extent to which the northern kingdom's large Canaanite element's cultural influence may have estranged its Israelites from the Judahites by melting them into general Canaanite culture was consciously limited by the kingdom's express recognition, down to its bureaucracy, that it was composed of two ethnically and even physically separate communities. This evidence of two consciously separate communities is attested to by both early and recent archeologists, though they differ over which was headquartered where. Finkelstein & Silberman cite this evidence themselves, but they seem not to appreciate its contribution to the 'Israeliteness" of Israel:

"In particular, the large and vibrant Canaanite population that endured in the north had to be integrated into the administrative machinery of any full-fledged state. Even before the recent archeological discoveries, the unique demographic mix of the population of the northern kingdom, espe-

---

[27] Finkelstein & Silberman, p. 194

cially the relationship between Israelites and Canaanites, did not escape the attention of biblical scholars. On the basis of the biblical accounts of religious turmoil within the Omride kingdom, the German scholar Albrecht Alt suggested that the Omrides had developed a system of dual rule from their two main capitals, with Samaria functioning as a center for the Canaanite population and Jezreel serving as the capital for the northern Israelites. The recent archeological and historical findings indicate exactly the opposite. The Israelite population was actually concentrated in the hill country around Samaria, while Jezreel, in the heart of the fertile valley, was situated in a region of clear Canaanite cultural continuity. . . ."[28]

There's a double irony in that last quoted sentence,

"The Israelite population was actually concentrated in the hill country around Samaria, while Jezreel, in the heart of the fertile valley, was situated in a region of clear Canaanite cultural continuity"

re Finkelstein & Silberman's claimed impact of Israel's large Canaanite element. Not only [a] was there "dual rule" for two peoples, but [b] the ruling Israelites were still "concentrated in the hill country around Samaria," just where, per Finkelstein & Silberman, Israel's young Six Day War vet archeologists first found them:

"In the formerly sparsely populated highlands from the Judean hills in the south to the hills of Samaria in the north, far from the Canaanite cities that were in the process of collapse and disintegration, about two-hundred fifty hilltop communities suddenly sprang up. Here were the first Israelites." [emphasis added] [29]

For all the Canaanites in Israel, the Israelites were still Israelites.

[3] The earliest known prophets were Judahites who preached to the Israelites in the northern kingdom of Israel: Further evidence of the "Israeliteness" of Israel in Finkelstein & Silberman's own book is their recognition of the religious impact of the preachings of biblical prophets in both kingdoms:

"It [the reign of northern king Jeroboam II] is also the period when we have the first record of prophetic protest. The oracles of the prophets Amos and Hosea are the earliest preserved prophetic books, containing material that reflects the heyday of Jeroboam II. Their scathing denunciations of the corrupt and impious aristocracy of the north [where they preached] serve both to document the opulence of this era and to express for the first time ideas that would exert a profound effect on the crystallization of the Deuteronomistic [sic] theology." [30]

---

[28] Finkelstein & Silberman, p. 192
[29] Finkelstein & Silberman, p. 107
[30] Finkelstein & Silberman, p. 212

Finkelstein & Silberman describe Amos as a shepherd who wandered north from rural Judah, but whatever his social status or reason for preaching in Israel, "the oracles recorded in his name provide a searing condemnation of the lavish lifestyles and material reality of Israel's aristocracy in the eighth century BCE."[31]

But they do more than that. Even in the brief excerpts from Amos that Finkelstein & Silberman quote, the prophet referred to "David" by only that name, and to prohibitions against work on the new moon and sabbath by just implication ("When will the new moon be over that we may sell grain? And the sabbath, that we may offer wheat for sale"). None of this would have been comprehensible, let alone meaningful, had there been no pan-Israelite historical and theological linkage between north and south.

And the preachings of Amos and Hosea in the north expressed the Israeliteness of what went on in the northern kingdom even more profoundly than that. In Finkelstein & Silberman's words, their preachings in the north "express for the first time ideas that would exert a profound effect on the crystallization of the Deuteronomistic [sic, i.e., Israeliteness "as we understand it from the perspective of the later biblical writers"] theology."[32]

[4] <u>Kinship links survived the destruction of Israel</u>. And there was a final, post-Israel link. When Israel was destroyed by the Assyrians in 722, it was to Judah that a "flow of refugees" fled.[33] But even more tellingly, it appears that the Assyrian-imposed population exchange, wherein Israelites were dispersed and foreigners brought in, was "far from total," and the subsequent relationship between Judah and the Israelites remaining in the north was based on unique common theology: Finkelstein & Silbeman:

"Indeed, surveys and excavations in the Jezreel valley confirm the surprising demographic continuity. And about half of the rural sites near Samaria continued to be occupied in subsequent centuries. We may even have a biblical reference to this demographic situation. A few years after the destruction of the northern kingdom, the Judahite king Hezekiah celebrated the Passover in Jerusalem. He reportedly 'sent to all Israel and Judah, and wrote letters also to Ephraim and Manasseh, that they

---

[31] Finkelstein & Silberman, pp. 212-213
[32] Finkelstein & Silberman, p. 212
[33] Finkelstein & Silberman, p. 223. See also Finkelstein & Silberman, pp. 247-248, on the religious impact on Judah of northern Israelites during and after the northern kingdom's final days.

36

should come to the house of the Lord at Jerusalem, to keep the passover to the Lord the God of Israel' (2 Chronicles 30:1). Ephraim and Manasseh refer to the highlands of Samaria to the north of Judah. While the historicity of Chronicles may be questioned, Jeremiah also reports, about 150 [sic] years after the fall of the northern kingdom, that Israelites from Shechem, Shiloh, and Samaria came with offerings to the Temple in Jerusalem (Jeremiah 41:5)." [34]

[5] Ezekiel evidences even a final post-Judah link. According to an Irish cleric Hebrew Testament scholar, it is "probable" that when Judahites were deported to Babylon they came into contact with descendants of the Israelites there, and that Ezekial exercised a common ministry amongst them.

" . . . the dead and dismembered bones can only refer to the divided and defunct kingdoms of Israel and Judah, while the simile of the revivification of thesebones signifies the ultimate resurgence and reunion of both kingdoms: 'Son of man, these bones are the whole house of Israel . . . I will . . . cause you to come up out of your graves, O my people; and I will bring you to the land of Israel' (vv. 11-12). The simile of the joined sticks in verses 15 f. continues this same theme: 'Behold I will take the stick of Joseph, which is the hand of Ephraim, and the tribes of Israel, and I will put them with it even the stick of Judah and make them one stick and they shall bo one in mine hand' (v. 19). Only an audience composed of representatives of both the Israelite and Judahite peoples could have provided the immediate background of these words of Ezekiel." [35]

2.3.2   The Southern Kingdom of Judah

According to Finkelstein & Silberman, "it was only after the fall of Israel that Judah grew into a fully developed state." But then, "something extraordinary happened." Judah's population swelled. It engaged in international trade. And the Bible was written.[36]

"Suddenly, at the end of the eighth century BCE, Jerusalem underwent an unprecedented population explosion, with its residential areas expanding from its former narrow ridge – the city of David – to cover the entire western hill . . . . In a matter of a few decades – surely within a single generation – Jerusalem was transformed from a modest highland town of about ten or twelve acres to a huge urban area of 150 acres of closely packed houses, workshops, and public buildings. In demographic terms, the city's population may have increased as much as fifteen times, from about one thousand to fifteen thousand inhabitants." [37]

---

[34] Finkelstein & Silberman, pp. 221-222

[35] Whitley, pp. 76-78

[36] Finkelstein & Silberman, pp. 229-230

[37] Finkelstein & Silberman, p. 243

Rural population growth and other signs of "mature state formation" appeared, which Finkelstein & Silberman attribute to Judah's economic and political integration into the Assyrian world.[38] And here, in the model of Finkelstein & Silberman, we come to the crux of the matter from the standpoint of Jewish history:

"Sometime in the late eighth century BCE there arose an increasingly vocal school of thought that insisted that the cults of the countryside were sinful –and that YHWH alone should be worshipped. We cannot be sure where the idea originated. It is expressed in the cycle of stories of Elijah and Elisha (set down in writing long after the fall of the Omrides) and, more important, in the works of the prophets Amos and Hosea, both of whom were active in the eighth century in the north. As a result, some biblical scholars have suggested that this movement originated among dissident priests and prophets in the last days of the northern kingdom who were aghast at the idolatry and social injustice of the Assyrian period. After the destruction of the kingdom of Israel, they fled southward to promulgate their ideas. Other scholars have pointed to circles connected with the Temple of Jerusalem intent on exercising religious and economic control over then increasingly developed countryside. Perhaps both factors played a part in the close-packed atmosphere of Jerusalem after the fall of Samaria, when refugees from the north and Judahite priests and royal officials worked together." [39]

So was born the "YHWH-alone movement." intent on creating "an unquestioned orthodoxy of worship – and a single, Jerusalem-centered national history. And it succeeded brilliantly in the crafting of what would become the laws of Deuteronomy and the Deuteronomistic History," and in triumphing over existing non-exclusively YHWH religious beliefs. Had the supporters of mixed YHWH and Canaanite deity worship won out, "we might have possessed an entirely different scripture – or perhaps none at all."[40]

Finkelstein & Silberman cite reforms toward YHYH-alone mentioned in Kings in King Asa's early 9th century time, but question that book's reliability.[41] It was in Hezekiah's time, 727-698 BCE, that the YHWH-alone movement matured, but even then the extent to which it took hold is not clear. King Hezekiah's accession to the throne of Judah in the late 8th century "was remembered by

---

[38] Finkelstein & Silberman, pp. 243-246
[39] Finkelstein & Silberman, pp. 247-248
[40] Finkelstein & Silberman, p. 248
[41] Finkelstein & Silberman, p. 249

the authors of the books of Kings as an event without precedent."[42] His ultimate goal was exclusive worship of YHWH exclusively in the Jerusalem Temple. "Hezekiah's religious reforms are difficult to detect in the archeological record. . . . Yet there is no question that by the reign of King Hezekiah, a profound change had come over the land of Judah. Judah was now the center of the people of Israel. Jerusalem was the center of the worship of YHWH. And the members of the Davidic dynasty were the only legitimate representatives and agents of YHWH's rule on earth."[43]

Kings and Chronicles recount Hezekiah's rebellion against the Assyrian overlords who had finished off Israel. Ironically, it is in this military, not religious, realm that Bible-confirming extrabiblical evidence abounds. "While there are only meager and disputed archeological indications for Hezekiah's religious reforms throughout his kingdom, there is abundant evidence for both the planning and the ghastly outcome of his revolt against Assyria."[44]

Hezekiah's revolt preparation included thickening Jerusalem walls, apparently those for which the prophet Isaiah castigated the king for having strengthened by breaking down houses, and the excavation of the famous water tunnel referred to in Chronicles and Kings. Earlier tunneling efforts had been directed to providing access to Jerusalem's crucial water source outside the walls. Hezekiah tunneled to bring the water inside. The celebrated stone "Siloam inscription" found in 1880 on the tunnel's wall captured the moment when the teams digging from opposite ends finally met. Finkelstein & Silberman declared that this extraordinary engineering achievement – recorded in Kings as Hezekiah having "made the pool and the conduit and brought water into the city" – "represents one of the rare instances when a specific project of a Hebrew king can safely be identified archeologically."[45]

---

[42] Finkelstein & Silberman, p. 249
[43] Finkelstein & Silberman, p. 250
[44] Finkelstein & Silberman, p. 255
[45] Finkelstein & Silberman, pp. 255-258. The famous mid-20th century guide writer Vilnay had likewise taken the "still extant" tunnel as confirming the Bible: "In Biblical times this spring lay outside the city precincts, beyond the wall, and so when the city was besieged the inhabitants were in danger of being cut off from their water supply. Therefore, about 700 B.C., King Hezekiah had a tunnel bored from the spring to the Pool of Siloam which was in Jerusalem proper. This

But King Hezekiah's name is not mentioned in the inscription. So is the tunnel accessible to tourists today really the work of the workmen of King Hezekiah of Judah two thousand eight hundred years earlier? *Compu-Serve News,* 3/7/2005:

"The Siloam Tunnel in that city [Jerusalem] matches the description of King Hezekiah's tunnel. But is it really the same one? That question has stumped scholars for years, many of whom insisted the Siloam Tunnel was built centuries later than the Bible suggested in Kings and Chronicles. The only clue that survived for more than 2,700 years is an inscription discovered in 1880 on a tunnel wall that supported the link to King Hezekiah, although it did not name him specifically, reports the Associated Press.

"Now geologists from the Cave Research Center at Hebrew University in Jerusalem think they have solved the mystery. By using radiocarbon testing to analyze the age of stalactite samples from the ceiling of the Siloam Tunnel and plant material recovered from its plaster floor, the biblical record and the tunnel's age have been confirmed, the researchers wrote in the journal Nature. The Siloam Tunnel is the one built by King Hezekiah."[46]

"Never before had a Judahite king devoted so much energy and expertise and so many resources in preparation for war." Outside Jerusalem, Lachish was surrounded by a formidable fortification system. Mass produced large storage jars for provisions, marked

---

important work is highly praised in the Bible." Vilnay, p. 161.

[46] Further evidence of Hezekiah's water-system building has been discovered in 2005. On August 9, 2005, the Israel Government Press Office released a report, "Monumental Water System of Biblical Times Uncovered By Archeologists Near Jerusalem," dating from the time of King Hezekiah, connected to the cave discovered last year that may have been used by John the Baptist. "Pottery finds from the site show that the entire water system was built in the eighth century B.C. at the time of King Hezekiah, at the same time as the hewing of the famous Siloam Tunnel in Jerusalem." The University of North Carolina archeologists who conducted the excavations called the massive enterprise "amazing."

And as with other biblical sites, there's a tie-in between biblical eras. On August 10, 2005, the Los Angeles Times reported the discovery of the biblical Pool of Siloam, near the c. 400 CE Byzantine one previously discovered. The LA Times reported:

"Workers repairing a sewage pipe in the old city of Jerusalem have discovered the biblical Pool of Siloam, a freshwater reservoir that was a major gathering place for ancient Jews making religious pilgrimages to the city and the reputed site where Jesus cured a man blind from birth, according to the gospel of John.

"The pool was fed by the now famous Hezekiah's Tunnel . . . ."

with an emblem believed to be a royal insignia and the Hebrew inscription "lmlk" ("belonging to the king"), and the name of one of four cities – Hebron, Socoh, Ziph, and an unidentified "MMST" – have been found. Their specific use has been debated, but "it is quite clear that they were associated with the organization of Judah before the rebellion against Assyria."[47]

In the event, the decision to revolt proved disastrous. Hezekiah's Judah proved no battlefield match for Sennacherib's Assyrians. "Despite the biblical report of the miraculous deliverance of Jerusalem, contemporary Assyrian records provide a very different picture of the outcome of Hezekiah's revolt." The Assyrian account begins "As to Hezekiah the Judahite, he did not submit to my yoke," proceeds to describe a swath of destruction through Judah, the taking of 200,000 human captives and animals "beyond counting," and "himself, I made prisoner in Jerusalem, his royal residence, like a bird in a cage." A huge 60' long, 9' high wall relief vividly illustrating the Assyrian siege of Lachish was discovered in the 1840's in Sennacherib's palace in Ninevah. It's inscribed: "Sennacherib, king of all, king of Assyria, sitting on his throne while the spoil from the city of Lachish passed before him." Is this mural for real, and is it the Judahite city Lachish?

"Some scholars have questioned the accuracy of the details of this relief and have argued that this is self-serving imperial propaganda, not a reliable record of what happened in Lachish. But there is hardly a doubt that the relief deals with the specific city of Lachish and with the specific events of 701 BCE. Not only are the topography of the city and the local vegetation represented accurately; it is even possible to identify the precise vantage point of the artist who made the sketch for the relief. Furthermore, the archeological excavations at Lachish have provided details about the location of the gate and the nature of the fortifications and the siege system that confirm the accuracy of the relief." [48]

Only Jerusalem and adjacent Judean hills were spared. "For all the Bible's talk of Hezekiah's piety and YHWH's saving intervention, Assyria was the sole victor. Sennacherib achieved his aims: he broke Judah's resistance and subjugated it. Hezekiah had inherited a prosperous state, and Sennacherib destroyed it."[49] Hezekiah's son and successor, biblically-vilified Manasseh, restored the

---

[47] Finkelstein & Silberman, pp. 257-259
[48] Finkelstein & Silberman, p. 262
[49] Finkelstein & Silberman, p. 264

economy and worship at high places. Alongside YHWH, "the cults of Baal, Asherah, and the host of heaven returned."[50]

Manasseh died in 642, succeeded by son Amon, who "did what was evil in the sight of the Lord, as Manasseh his father had done" (2 Kings 21). He was soon assassinated, but the people slew the conspirators and put his young son Josiah on the throne, who ruled 31 years, praised by the Bible as "the most righteous king in the history of Judah, rivaling the reputation of even David himself."[51]

"This time, too, their passionate religious convictions and single-minded vision of the power of YHWH to protect Judah and the Davidic dynasty against all earthly opponents would founder on the hard realities of history. But this time they would leave behind them a brilliant testament that would keep their ideas alive. Their great monument would be a timeless collection of Hebrew texts expressing their view of history and their hopes for the future. That collective saga would be the unshakable foundation for the Hebrew Bible we know today." [52]

Finkelstein & Silberman argue Assyria's decline and resurgent Egypt's preoccupation with the coastal plain left the way open for Judah to expand and take over the territories of the old northern kingdom and create a "pan-Israelite state." But "such an ambitious plan would require active and powerful propaganda."[53] And this, they said, is the genesis of "the dramatic surfacing of a text,"[54] found by the high priest during Temple renovations, long recognized as the source document of Deuteronomy. "Its impact was enormous, for it suddenly and shockingly revealed that the traditional practice of the cult of YHWH in Judah had been wrong."[55]

Josiah gathered the people of Judah and had them "conclude a solemn oath to devote themselves entire to the divine commandments detailed in the newly discovered book." He "launched the most intense puritan reform in the history of Judah." 2 Kings 23:4-7 records he removed from the Temple "all the vessels made for Baal, for Asherah, and for all the host of heaven," deposed idolatrous priests, and eradicated foreign cult shrines reportedly established under royal patronage in Jerusalem as early as Solomon's

---

[50] Finkelstein & Silberman, p. 265
[51] Finkelstein & Silberman, p. 273
[52] Finkelstein & Silberman, pp. 273-274
[53] Finkelstein & Silberman, p. 283
[54] Finkelstein & Silberman, p. 277
[55] Finkelstein & Silberman, pp. 276-277

lem's walls. He instituted social legislation aiding the poor, and he too forbade intermarrying with foreign wives.[11]

"These rulings by Ezra and Nehemiah in Jerusalem in the fifth century BCE laid the foundations for Second Temple Judaism in the establishment of clear boundaries between the Jewish people and their neighbors and in the strict enforcement of the Deuteronomic Law. Their efforts – and the efforts of other Judean priests and scribes which took place over the one hundred and fifty years of exile, suffering and soul-searching, and political rehabilitation – led to the birth of the Hebrew Bible in its substantially final form." [12]

That final form was affected by need to make sense of the trauma that had transpired. The thrust of pre-exilic Deuteronomistic History had been that Josiah's piousness and reforms centralizing worship in the Jerusalem Temple had secured preservation of Judah under the Davidic line. Now all that lay in ruins. What future now remained? The Bible editors' solution, say Finkelstein & Silberman, citing American biblical scholar Frank Moore Cross and his school, is that the Deuteronomistic History went through two, pre- and post-exilic, redactions, Dtr[1] and Dtr[2]. The post-exilic revision shifted righteousness responsibility from the king to all the people, and credited Josiah's righteousness, following Manassah's evils, as sufficient only to put the day of the Lord's vengeance off. This is seen in the "chilling oracle" that the post-exilic redaction "placed in the mouth of Huldah the prophetess," and other passages. Thus, "the second Deuteronomist left a future for Israel even without a king, and for good measure wrote of the release of King Johoiachin from prison in Baghdad as well."[13]

3.2.4   Life, Political Rule and Religious Leadership In Yehud

"The Persian takeover and the return of a certain number of exiles who were supported by the Persian government changed the settlement situation there. Urban life in Jerusalem began to revive and many returnees settled in the Judean hills. . . . Survey data from all the settlements in Yehud in the fifth-fourth centuries BCE yields a population of approximately thirty thousand people . . . . This small number constituted the post-exilic community of the time of Ezra and Nehemiah so formative in shaping later Judaism." [14]

---

[11] Finkelstein & Silberman, pp. 300-301

[12] Finkelstein & Silberman, p. 301

[13] Finkelstein & Silberman, pp. 303-305

[14] Finkelstein & Silberman, pp. 307-308

time. He ended sacrifice at the scattered countryside high places and shrines, destroyed the old northern altar at Bethel, and removed (2 Kings 23:19-20) all the shrines of the high places in the cities of Samaria, "which kings of Israel had made, provoking the Lord to anger."[56] But, he decreed (2 Kings 23:21-23):

"'Keep the passover to the Lord your God, as it is written in this book of the covenant.' For no such passover had been kept since the days of the judges who judged Israel, or during all the days of the kings of Israel or of the kings of Judah; but in the eighteenth year of king Josiah this passover was kept to the Lord in Jerusalem."

There was another facet, reverberating down the ages as well.

"Deuteronomy contains ethical laws and provisions for social welfare that have no parallel anywhere else in the Bible. Deuteronomy calls for the protection of the individual, for the defense of what we would call today human rights and human dignity. Its laws offer unprecedented concern for the weak and helpless within Judahite society. . . . This was not to be a matter of mere charity, but a consciousness that grew out of the shared perception of nationhood, now strongly reinforced by the historical saga of Israel, codified in text."[57]

But perhaps Josiah's time was not ethical concerns' earliest expression Hebrew. The 1/8/10 *Jerusalem Post* carried a highly speculative, highly criticized translation of the Elah ostracon expressing such ethical concerns at the time of King David.[58]

Yet archeological support for Josiah's reforms is weak. Figurines of a woman identified as the goddess Asherah, have been widely found in private dwellings throughout late 7th century Judah.[59]

Josiah was killed, perhaps in battle, by Egyptian king Necho at Megiddo in 609. "Decades of spiritual revival and visionary hopes seemingly collapsed overnight. Josiah was dead and the

---

[56] Finkelstein & Silberman, pp. 277-279

[57] Finkelstein & Silberman, p. 285

[58] Haifa University Prof. Gershon Galil's controversial decipherment of the Elah Fortress pottery shard. In English translation it says:
1: "you shall not do [it], but worship the [Lord]"
2: "Judge the sla[ve] and the wid[ow] / judge the orph[an]"
3: "[and] the stranger. [P]lead for the infant / plead for the po[or and]"
4: "the widow. Rehabilitate [the poor] at the hands of the king."
5: "Protect the po[or and] the slave / [supp]ort the stranger."
(Jerusalem Post, 1/8/10, "Inscription Indicates Kingdom of Israel Existed in the 10th Century BCE.")

[59] Finkelstein & Silberman, pp. 287-288

43

people of Israel were again enslaved by Egypt." The great reform movement apparently crumbled, and the final four kings of Judah are harshly judged by the Bible. Judah's last two decades are described by the Deuteronomistic History as "a period of continuous decline, leading to a destruction of the Judahite state."[60]

The end was not merciful. Egypt controlled the western part of the former Assyrian empire, advancing its dream of resurrecting pharaonic glory. But in Mesopotamia, Babylonian the power steadily grew. In 605, the Babylonian crown prince later known as Nebuchadnezzar crushed the Egyptians at Carchemish in Syria (an event recorded in Jeremiah 46:2), causing the Egyptian forces to flee back toward the Nile. The Assyrian empire was thus irrevocably dismembered, and Nebuchadnezzar, now king of Babylon, sought to gain complete control over all the lands to the west."[61]

"And so the Babylonian noose around Jerusalem tightened. The Babylonians were now intent on the plunder and complete destruction of the Judahite state." It was not long in coming. Both the Bible and Babylonian records describe the 597 siege and surrender of Jerusalem, the plunder of Temple and city, the taking away of King Jehoiachin, royal court, officials, aristocracy, priests, soldiers and craftsmen into exile as captives, and the installation by the Babylonian king of Johoiachin's uncle, Zedekiah, as vassal. But Zedekiah himself revolted, and "in 587 BCE Nebuchadnezzar arrived with his formidable army and laid siege to Jerusalem. It was the beginning of the end." The Babylonians rampaged through the countryside, and the cities of Judah fell one after another. "At Lashich in the Shephelah, ostraca found in the ruins of the last city gate offer a poignant glimpse of the last moments of the independence of Judah as the signal fires from the neighboring towns are snuffed out, one by one": "And may my lord know," an outpost officer wrote to his Lashich commander, "that we are watching for the signals of Lashich according to all the signs that my lord gave. For we do not see Azekah …."[62]

"Finally, all that was left was Jerusalem." Food in the besieged capital had run out. 2 Kings 25:3-7: "Then a breach was made in

---

[60] Finkelstein & Silberman, pp 289-292
[61] Finkelstein & Silberman, p. 292
[62] Finkelstein & Silberman, p. 294

the city; the king with all the men of war fled by night . . . . But the army of the Chaldeans pursued the king, and overtook him in the plains of Jericho; and all his army was scattered from him. Then they captured the king, and brought him up to the king of Babylon at Riblah, who passed sentence upon him. They slew the sons of Zedekiah before his eyes, and put out the eyes of Zedekiah, and bound him in fetters, and took him to Babylon."

A month later, a Babylonian captain and soldiers came to Jerusalem. 2 Kings 25:8-11: "And he burned the house of the Lord and the king's house and all the houses of Jerusalem . . . And all the army of the Chaldeans . . . broke down the walls around Jerusalem. And the rest of the people who were left in the city . . . Nebuzaradan the captain of the guard carried into exile."

Finkelstein & Silberman:

"And so it was all over. Four hundred years of Judah's history came to an end in fire and blood. The proud kingdom of Judah was utterly devastated, its economy ruined, its society ripped apart. The last king in a dynasty that had ruled for centuries was tortured and imprisoned in Babylon. His sons were all killed. The Temple of Jerusalem – the only legitimate place for the worship of YHWH – was destroyed.

"The religion and national existence of the people of Israel could have ended in this great disaster. Miraculously, both survived." [63]

---

[63] Finkelstein & Silberman, p. 295

45

Chapter 3
The Jews' Second Temple

3.1   Six Hundred Years In A Nutshell

The Kingdom of Judah's end at Babylonian hands in 586 BCE might have ended the Israelites as a people, but for multiple reasons did not. Not all were exiled; indeed, a majority (sic) remained on the land. The uprooted were sent together to Babylon, not scattered to the four winds, and there they retained their identity and even encountered their earlier exiled kinsmen from the old northern kingdom of Israel. Judah was not filled with newcomers from afar. And the exile did not last long. The Babylonians, like the Assyrians before them, did not long survive their conquering of a biblical kingdom, and Cyrus, the Persian king who but a generation later conquered the Babylonians in turn, and his successors, for their own reasons, issued decrees allowing the Jews to return. In waves of return, they merged with their countrymen who had remained on the Land, reinvigorated their old way of life and even, with the ruling Persians' cooperation, rebuilt their Temple.

We think of Israel and Judah with kings and prophets striding larger than life through the Bible as "biblical Israel." They were. But so too were Ezra and Nehemiah's and Second Temple Yehud and Judaea, where Jews compiled the Hebrew Bible we and the world know today. It was in Judaea, under pagan Rome, but while the Temple still stood, that Jesus lived and left his mark on the world.

The Jews' Second Temple stood for six centuries, as long as from the early hill settlements to the destruction of their First. The Second Temple entity too came face-to-face, again in the end cataclysmically, with ancient world mighty rulers – Persians, Alexander, his Ptolmaic and Seleucid successors, and finally Rome. The Second Temple era witnessed three of Jewish history's great wars: the successful Maccabean Revolt and the two failed Revolts against Rome. It must have seemed their world's end to much of the Great Revolt generation when Temple and State came crashing down. Indeed, many today believe that from then until the Zionist movement eighteen hundred years later, Jews were virtually absent from Palestine and played no meaningful part in its affairs. That isn't what happened at all. Within sixty years, the Jews in the Land, led by Bar Kochba, revolted again. Even after that final extinction of ancient sovereign Jewish independence in Israel, begun a millennium earlier, organized Jewish presence, the Yishuv, remained on The Land and, as with Assyrians and Babylonians, outlasted their Roman conquerors and their Byzantine heirs.

3.2 Yehud

3.2.1 The Majority that Remained On The Land

From Kings and Jeremiah, we've known that "the poorest of the land" were not deported to Babylon.[1] But we also know now from pre-deportation population estimates founded on those "intensive surveys and excavations" that it was not just the "poorest of the land" who remained. Finkelstein & Silberman:

"even if we accept [from biblical sources] the highest possible figures for exiles (twenty thousand), it would seem that they comprised at **most** [emphasis original] a quarter of the population of the Judahite state. That would mean that at least seventy-five percent of the population remained on the land."[2]

Thus, "both text and archeology contradict the idea that between the destruction of Jerusalem in 586 BCE and the return of the ex-

---

[1] Finkelstein & Silberman, pp. 297-298
[2] Finkelstein & Silberman, p. 306

47

iles after the proclamation of Cyrus in 538 BCE Judah was in total ruin and uninhabited."[3]

We know a little about those who remained. Jerusalem was destroyed, but Temple site cultic activity continued. See Jeremiah 41:5. There's evidence of continued habitation at Mizpah, "the most important settlement in the region in the sixth century BCE," and at Bethel, Gibeon and Bethlehem. "Thus, to both the north and south of Jerusalem, life continued almost interrupted."[4]

Of their government we know little. Babylon appointed one Gedaliah as governor at Mizpah, a haven for remaining Judahites, including Jeremiah. But he and officials were soon assassinated, apparently for cooperating with the conquerors and posing a threat to hopes of the Davidic line. Jeremiah and others fled to Egypt. Finkelstein & Silberman characterize their departure as "bringing to an apparent end centuries of Israelite occupation of the Promised Land,"[5] but their emphasis is on "apparent" rather than "end."

3.2.2   The Exiles

Ezekiel, written by an exiled Temple priest, and Second Isaiah (ch 40-55) shed light on the first generation in Babylon. They lived in both capital and countryside. Jeremiah had counseled them: "Build houses and live in them; plant gardens and eat their produce," to marry and raise families: "multiply there, and do not decrease."[6]

3.2.3   Return, Rebuilding the Temple, Constructing Dtr[2]

History soon took a turn. The Neo-Babylonian empire was conquered by Persia in 539 BCE. In the first year of his reign, Cyrus, the Persian empire's founder, issued a royal decree for the restoration of Judah and the Temple, recounted in Ezra (1:2-3). Sheshbazzar, called by Ezra "the prince of Judah," probably indicating that he was a son of exiled king Jehoiachin, led the first group of returnees, about 50,000 per Ezra. They resettled in their old homeland and laid the foundations for a new Temple. A few years later, a second group, led by an apparent grandson of Jehoiachin named Zerubbabel and a priest named Jeshua, followed, built

---

[3] Finkelstein & Silberman, p. 307
[4] Finkelstein & Silberman, p. 307
[5] Finkelstein & Silberman, pp. 297-298
[6] Finkelstein & Silberman, p. 298

an altar, celebrated the Feast of Tabernacles, and, as described in Ezra (3:11-13), began building the Temple.[7]

Ezra records that the people of Samaria, "the ex-citizens of the northern kingdom and the deportees who were brought there by the Assyrians," asked to join in the work, but that Jeshua and Zerubbabel rebuffed them: "You have nothing to do with us in building a house to our God." In resentment, these people hindered the work, and warned the Persian king that if the city and its walls were rebuilt, the Jews[8] would rebel and stop paying tribute. The king ordered a halt, but Zerubbabel and Jeshua did not stop, referring the Persian governor to Cyrus' original decree. The new king, Darius, confirmed this to the governor, ordering state subsidization and decreeing punishment of obstructers. "The construction of the Temple was then finished in the year 516 BCE. Thus began the era of Second Temple Judaism."[9]

A half-century of which we know little followed. Then Ezra the scribe came to Jerusalem from Babylon, c. 458 BCE, with more returnees, with judicial authority and a commission from the Persian king to inquire "about Judah and Jerusalem." Shocked by intermingling and inter-marriage of the people with others in the land, Ezra gathered "all the men of Judah and Benjamin" at Jerusalem, and (Ezra 10:9-16) demanded: "Now then make confession to the Lord the God of your fathers, and do his will; separate yourselves from the peoples of the land and from the foreign wives," which they did. And then Ezra, "one of the most influential figures of biblical times," disappeared from the scene.[10]

"The other hero of that time" was Nehemiah, the cupbearer or high court official of the Persian king. He heard of the desperate state of Judah's inhabitants and Jerusalem's terrible disrepair, and obtained Persian king Artaxerxes' permission to go to Jerusalem, to which he arrived as governor c. 445 BCE. He led a successful effort, despite neighboring peoples' opposition, to rebuild Jerusa-

---

[7] Finkelstein & Silberman, p. 299
[8] Following the destruction of the Temple and end of the kingdom of Judah, the conventional terminology is to refer to the former kingdom as the Persian province of "Yehud," and the Judahites as "Yehudim" or "Jews." Finkelstein & Silberman, p. 297.
[9] Finkelstein & Silberman, pp. 299-300
[10] Finkelstein & Silberman, p. 300

Less than fifty years passed between Judah's fall in 586 and Cyrus allowing return in 538. Many had never left, and the Temple was soon rebuilt, and in those senses Jewish connection to the Land continued from the old era into the new. But Yehud was not a continuation of Judah, though the people and their religious beliefs were the same. Persians acted in perceived Persian, not Judahite, interests. Return of displaced populations in their new empire, promoting their cults and granting autonomy was Persian policy, and in former Judah's case established a buffer near Egypt.

The returnees, though a minority in former Judah, rose to leadership through concentration at Jerusalem and religious, socioeconomic and political status. Apparent members of the Davidic line were among them, and like Sheshbazzar leaders in restoring Temple treasures and rebuilding the Temple. But unlike Judah, Yehud was ruled politically by Persian-appointed governors and religiously by the priesthood, which had risen to leadership during the Exile. "Lacking the institution of kingship, the Temple now became the center of identity of the people of Yehud. This was one of the most crucial turning points in Jewish history."[15]

3.3   Judea Under Alexander and His Successors

After two Persian-rule centuries, Alexander's conquests brought Yehud, which became Judaea, into his successors' empires, first that of the Ptolemies of Egypt, then of the Seleucids of Syria."[16]

When Alexander's armies marched into Yehud in 332 BCE, the implications for its Jews were profound. "With the Macedonian occupation, Israel was swept into the orbit of Hellenism, and came within range of the Greek writers and philosophers for the first time." The Ben-Gurion-edited *The Jews In Their Land* records that the Greeks were uncharacteristically impressed.[17]

Circa 300 BCE, the Greek writer Hecataeus of Abdera, who traveled Near East, wrote "the first extensive description of biblical laws and customs from an outside observer," providing "a glimpse of a stage of the Jewish tradition in which the prestige of the priesthood and the power of Deuteronomy's social legislation had

---

[15] Finkelstein & Silberman, p. 310
[16] Finkelstein & Silberman, p. 315
[17] JIL, pp. 122-123

completely overshadowed the tradition of the monarchy." All this Hecataeus attributed to laws established by "a man named Moses, outstanding for both his wisdom and courage."[18] He described how the Jews were ready to give their lives defending the Torah.[19]

"The Judeans, or Jews, became known throughout the Mediterranean as a community with a unique devotion to their God. At its heart were not only the shared law codes and rules of sacrifice, but the saga of national history that began with the call of Abraham in distant Ur and ended with the restoration of the Temple community by Ezra and Nehemiah in the post-exilic period. With the abandonment of the monarchy and the scattering of Jews throughout the Greco-Roman world, the sacred text of the Hebrew Bible was gradually translated into Greek in the third and second centuries BCE and became the chief source of community identity and guidance for all those members of the house of Israel who lived beyond the immediate vicinity of the Temple of Jerusalem. Its saga of the Exodus and the conquest of the Promised Land offered a shared vision of solidarity and hope for every individual in the community – in a way that royal or heroic mythologies could not." [20]

After Alexander died in 323, Ptolemy marched into Jerusalem, which had "a very large population – far larger than it had in the time of Nehemiah," on the Sabbath, with dreadful result. "Meticulous observance of the Sabbath rest by the Jews of Jerusalem was responsible for their failure to resist." Ptolemy "ruthlessly . . . carried many Jews off as captives to Egypt."[21]

In 200 BCE, the Seleucids defeated the Ptolemies in Syria, and in battles in Judaea and Jerusalem obtained control of all Judaea.[22] Not for the last time in their history, the Land's Jews aided the new foreign invader, helping oust the old, and not for the last time the new ruler's rewards for their aid proved fleeting indeed.

"The help given to [Seleucid ruler] Antiochus' forces by the Judaeans was considerable. They provided supplies . . . they drove the Egyptian garrison from its Jerusalem fortress, and greeted the triumphant Seleucid troops in Jerusalem with great enthusiasm. In recognition of this support, Antiochus authorized . . . the distribution of funds to maintain Temple worship and refurbish the sanctuary . . . and made other concessions. . . .

---

[18] Finkelstein & Silberman, p. 315
[19] JIL, p. 123. Demetrius of Phaleron, famous as an Athenian statesman and distinguished student of Aristotle's successor, was greatly fascinated by Jews' history, philosophy and Bible. Ibid.
[20] Finkelstein & Silberman, p. 316
[21] JIL, p. 124
[22] JIL, p. 128

And most important of all, the main clause of a royal charter approved Judaea's laws as the legal code of the Land: 'All the people shall determine their form of government in accordance with the laws of their forefathers.' Judaea, with its juridical and social system resting solidly upon the Torah, had received official endorsement of its regime from Persia in Ezra's days, and the Ptolemies had followed that policy scrupulously. Now, with the Seleucids in control of Judaea, its laws were affirmed for the third time."[23]

3.4 Independent Judaea Under the Maccabee-Hasmoneans

3.4.1 The Sparking of the Rebellion

Antiochus III's successor, Seleucus IV (187-175 BCE) maintained these policies. Change occurred under Antiochus Epiphanies (Antiochus IV, 175-164 BCE), regarded as an arch-villain in Jewish history for desecrating the Temple and seeking to stamp out Jews' ancient religious beliefs. In fact, the "change in policy" under him was "the outcome of a complex of internal events that were aggravated, in turn, by external involvements."[24] The "internal events" were feuds within the Jewish elite and between them and the populace over Hellenizing, control of Temple funds, local government and other matters.[25] The "external involvements" were the Seleucids' running conflicts with the Egypt-based Ptolemies.

"Matters came to a head" when Antiochus sought to build a Jerusalem fortress as a defense against Egypt and to keep control of Judaea. Work commenced, intentionally, on the Sabbath and, contrary to what the Seleucids' expected, the Jews rioted. This was the spark, but the fuel had been stacked and waiting. Earlier rioting had followed discovery that jigh priest Menelaus had sold gold vessels of the Temple. "This," the JIL authors wrote,

"was the beginning of fierce civil strife – still confined to Jerusalem, but already charged with the explosive ingredients that Seleucid interference in Judaea's affairs was about to ignite. And the blaze came soon enough when the Yishuv declared open war – not just on a faction of [Hellenizing] reformers, but on the whole of the Seleucid Empire."[26]

The "defenders of the Torah's sovereignty," conducting guerrilla operations, rapidly gained support. The Seleucids soon realized

---

[23] Jil, p. 128
[24] JIL, p. 128
[25] See JIL, pp. 128-130
[26] JIL, pp. 130-131

"they would have to declare war on the principal source of mischief – the religion of Israel. The text of Antiochus Epiphanes' proclamation can have differed very little, if at all, from the account given in the First Book of Maccabees (1:41 et seq). In general terms, the proclamation forbade any nation of the empire to set itself apart, to disassociate itself from the other nations."[27]

The Seleucids appreciated but "vaguely" the numbers and intensity of Judaeans willing to die for their Torah. Others in the empire "easily identified" their gods with the Greeks'. Not the Judaeans, save for the Jason-Menelaus faction anxious "to break down the 'separatism' taught in the Bible." The Seleucids, using forces already in Judaea, launched "a series of victorious attacks against the Yishuv." But these military successes led to sacrilege.

"On the 25th of the Hebrew month of Kislev, 167 B.C.E., an 'abomination of desolation' was placed on the altar of the Temple: in the Lord's sanctuary, in Holy Jerusalem, the graven image of an earth-bound 'god of the skies' (Zeus) was set up, and the heathens of the empire came to pay homage to it. . . . This act was the prelude to fresh Seleucid oppressions, known collectively as the 'Antiochean decrees.' The decrees forbade compliance with the laws of the Torah – including observance of the Sabbath, and circumcision – on pain of death. Jews everywhere were compelled to take part in idolatrous worship and to offer up sacrifices onaltars erected for the purpose. Some submitted to the decrees; others fled to the desert. Many suffered martyrdom rather than violate the Torah's decrees."[28]

3.4.2 The Maccabean Revolt

The rebels united under Mattathias, a priest of the Hasmonean house of Modi'in. With Hasidims' assent, the Jews abandoned the disastrous policy not to fight on the Sabbath. On Mattathias' death, one of his sons, Judas, known as Maccabeus, became leader. His first clash was with the attacking Appolonius, governor of Samaria, who was killed and his forces routed. A second Seleucid attack was repulsed. Judas then surprise-attacked a third Seleucid force while its general was off hunting, forcing him to retreat through hostile Jewish country, suffering disastrous losses and reaping the Jewish guerrillas enormous war booty enabling them to organize a regular army.[29]

---

[27] JIL, p. 132

[28] JIL, p. 132

[29] JIL, pp. 132-134

A regular army, but not a world-class one of the caliber of the imperial successors of Alexander The Great. Still, Judas extended Judaea's bounds, annexing to it Hebron and areas of dense Jewish settlement in the south and mixed in the west, and defended Jews in gentile towns. "But it was the political consequences of his victories that mattered most." After yet another Seleucid force was likewise routed, with the Seleucids engaged on another front, in bad financial straits, and with Rome threatening to intervene, the Seleucids decided upon a political resolution with Judaea's Jews. "In the spring of 164 B.C.E., all previous dictates against Judaism were withdrawn, and all insurgents who returned to their normal occupations within a fortnight were granted a free pardon."[30]

But it was now too late. The Jews' representative in the negotiations on rescinding the anti-Jewish decrees had been Menelaus,

"and Judas Maccabaeus and his followers – distrusting the Seleucid promises – would not disarm. Instead, Judas marched on Jerusalem at the head of his forces, taking the city (but not the citadel) in 164 B.C.E. Three years after its pollution, Judas and his men were able to cleanse the Temple, and in memory of its rededication the festival of Hanuka was established for all generations." [31]

That action made Judas the recognized head of Judaea. After a year's further fighting in border regions, he readied for an attack on the Seleucid-held citadel in Jerusalem, a direct challenge to the Seleucids themselves. But instead of deploying the empire's full military force against Judas, in an all-out campaign in which the JIL author affirmed the empire "would have undoubtedly been victorious," the Seleucids, "displaying remarkable diplomatic skill," restored to the Yishuv "all the rights it had enjoyed under Antiochus III, thus reversing the Jason-Menelaus reforms. Menelaus was condemned as a traitor to the empire, and put to death. Judas was not touched, the fortress in Jerusalem remained," and a new high priest, Alcimus, to the Seleucids' liking, was installed.[32]

That might have ended the Maccabean adventure, but a 162 Seleucid coup brought a new ruler, Demetrius I, to the throne, who supported Alcimus against Judas, reuniting the people behind him. In a new battle against Seleucid forces Judas won again. Then, in an

---

[30] JIL, p. 134
[31] JIL, p. 134
[32] JIL, pp. 134-136

effort to rid The Land of Seleucid control, Judas in 161 BCE concluded an alliance with Rome. A mighty Seleucid army invaded. In the ensuing battle Judas was killed. With Alcimus' support, the Seleucids ringed the country with forts and began a campaign of oppression. But Judas' brothers organized Judean desert resistance, which the Seleucids failed despite repeated efforts to crush. Eventually the Seleucids, "despairing now of victory, accepted that the only real power was in Hasmonean hands."[33]

Judas' brother Jonathan, as military leader and high priest, expanded Judaea's borders and influence. After his murder by a Syrian general, another brother, Simeon, succeeding him, took the citadels in Jerusalem and elsewhere, and expelled foreigners from Jaffa and made it the main Jewish port.[34] Then came events of great historic significance:

"In 142 B.C.E. the independence of Judaea was recognized by Demetrius II. The climax came on the 18th of the Hebrew month of Elul, 140 B.C.E. On that day, before priests and people, leaders and elders, Simeon was proclaimed hereditary nassi (prince or president), high priest, and commander in chief, and was entrusted with all the concerns of the Temple and the Land. . . . So a new royal dynasty, the house of the Hasmoneans, was born. Once again the Yishuv could enjoy political independence. Simeon's appointment as nassi and high priest was for life – or until 'a prophet of truth should arise in Israel.' This exceptional proviso admitted an awareness that the full sovereignty enjoyed by Judaea fell short of perfection, and that the privileges vouchsafed to Simeon by the Great Convocation – especially in respect to his double title – were not to be thought of as equaling God's promise to David that his house should reign in perpetuity."[35]

Remarkable.

3.4.3   The Hasmonean State

Judaea was not alone. Dynastic struggles sapped Seleucids' strength and their empire disintegrated, collapsing completely on the death of its last great king in 129. Johanan Hyrcanus (135-104), son and heir of Simeon, wrested control of the entire Land.

"Johanan's military campaigns were conducted on three fronts – in the north, south and east – and proved of major importance for the country's future. In the first 20 years of the second century B.C.E., he succeeded in

---

[33] JIL, p. 136
[34] JIL, p. 136
[35] JIL, pp. 136-137

annexing important areas in the interior of the Judaean state. Of particular importance was his expansion to the south: the whole of Idumea (Edom) became a part of Judaea and its inhabitants were converted to Judaism. From then on, the Idumeans were an inseparable part of the Jewish nation, and their leading families occupied positions of authority in the Hasmonean state. Johanan also made conquests in Transjordan and advanced in the direction of Samaria, occupying the Samaritan center at Shechem and destroying their temple on Mount Gerezim." [36]

The Judaeans weren't done. Johanan went on to capture the Hellenistic cities Samaria and Scythopolis (Beit-She'an), and began taking the Galilee. His son Aristobulus I (104-103) completed occupation of Galilee and converted the Itureans to Judaism. All this was facilitated by ties with Rome, established by Judas Maccabaeus and furthered by Johanan Hyrancus and with other powers. [37]

Aristobulus' brief reign was followed by the long one of his brother, Alexander Jannaeus (103-76 BCE), under whom "the Jewish kingdom of this Second Temple period grew as large as it was ever to be." He took Gaza after strong resistance and cities in Transjordan and around the Kinneret (Sea of Galilee). He was succeeded by his wife, Alexandra (76-67 BCE). Her rate of conquest was slower, and an abortive attempt to take Damascus actually endangered Judaea when Armenia invaded Syria and approached Judaea's borders, but was checked when Rome invaded Armenia. "From that point on, the Land of Israel, together with Syria, entered into the sphere of direct Roman expansion." [38]

The JIL author summarized the Hasmoneans' accomplishments:

"The Hasmonean conquests in effect halted the Greek domination of the Land and blocked the expansion of the Hellenistic cities and the mixed Semitic-Greek elements into the interior. Thanks to the success of the Hasmoneans' political policies, most of the country's Semitic inhabitants became part of the Jewish nation, and the islands of Jewish settlement scattered throughout the Land became part of the Jewish state. The name 'Judaea' ceased to apply only to a limited area around Jerusalem; in this period it became the name of the entire Land of Israel. (It was still the official name of the country when Hadrian ruled in the second century C.E.) The new name reflected the ethnic changes and the relations of forces established during the period of the Hasmonean conquests. The territorial expansion had been gradual, until Johanan Hyrcanus and Alexander Jannaeus finally broke the back of the Hellenistic cities: through

---

[36] JIL, pp. 137-138
[37] JIL, pp. 138-139
[38] JIL, pp. 139-140

their victories, the Jews became a majority again in the Land; and they remained one even after the collapse of the Hasmonean state." [39]

The people's decision of 142 BCE, investing Simeon with the titles of high priest, nassi and military commander, commenced Hasmoneans' dynastic rule. They clung to the high priesthood, the most important title since Persian rule, but assumed the title of ethnarch in dealing with foreign powers. "The radical change took place only in the days of Aristobulus I, who assumed the kingly crown to increase the prestige of the Hasmonean rulers." Gradually, Hasmonean rulership morphed from "the holiness and dedication to a cause that had been evident under Judas Maccabaeus and his brothers" into a royal court resembling "in manners, atmosphere, and external splendor, the courts of the other kings of the east." They fortified their towns – "Jerusalem, the capital, was known as an unusually strong city, and the Temple Mount within it was evidently a fortified area on its own" – and their military prowess was noted internationally, including by the Greek writer Strabo. Hellenization was present, evidenced by the rulers' adoption of Greek names in addition to their Hebrew ones, but "the fundamentally Jewish character of the kingdom – the product of a desperate religious war" – remained. [40]

"The establishment of the Hasmonean state strengthened the status of the many Jewish communities of the Diaspora – those communities living in foreign lands, whose roots went back many generations. Hundreds of thousands of Jews continued to live in Mesoptamia and throughout the Mediterranean world." Agriculture remained the basis of Judaea's economy, but commerce and trade through the country's ports became large-scale, and Judaeans were "prominent in the commercial affairs of Delos and Athens." [41]

There evolved during Hasmonean times the two sects that "left their imprint on all the inner development of Judaea during the Second Temple period: the Pharisees and the Sadducees." The Pharisees, whose great sages the people regarded as their teachers and guides, popularized the Torah and upheld the oral law. The Sadducees, aristocrats from families close to the pre-Hasmonean high priesthood, opposed oral law as equal to written. They were a

---

[39] JIL, p. 140

[40] JIL, pp. 140-141

[41] JIL, pp. 141-142

minority, but extremely powerful due to social standing and wealth. There were other sects, including the ascetic Essenes, "but the main struggle for the soul of the nation and the character of the state was conducted between the Pharisees and the Sadducees."[42]

3.5   Roman Rule

3.5.1   The Arrival of Rome

Most Westerners know of the Temple's destruction and Massada siege during the Jews' Great Revolt against Rome, and many of the Jews' fleetingly successful second, Bar Kochba, revolt. But "revolt," successful or not, is waged against foreign rule. Less known is how Judaea fell to Rome, though the stage is replete with Roman players as famous as any personalities of ancient times.

"When the Romans appeared in Syria in 64 B.C.E. the political situation in the Land was already unsteady. Once Pompey, the Roman commander, decided to annex Syria, Roman intervention in Judaea became inevitable. The bitter struggle that broke out after the death of Alexandra between her two sons, Hyrcanus and Aristobulus, did no more than hasten this intervention and – to some extent – affect its character. Pompey decided in favor of Hyrcanus, whose supporters opened the gates of Jerusalem to the Romans; but he met determined resistance from Aristobulus' army on the Temple Mount. After a three months' siege, in which thousands of the defenders were killed, the Temple fortress was taken, and in 63 B.C.E. the whole of Judaea was absorbed into the political framework of the Roman Republic. Thus ended one of the most glorious periods in Israel's history. The Hasmonean State had maintained its independence for some 80 years, and in that time it had succeeded in consolidating the Land of Israel under Jewish rule." [43]

Unlike Syria, reduced to a province, Pompey allowed Judaea autonomy, but ports and parts of Idumea and Samaria were lost to it. Hyrcanus II was put in charge. Then Judaea became embroiled in one of history's clashes of giants – that of Caesar and Pompey.

"Under Julius Caesar (who ruled Judaea from 4544 B.C.E.) there was some improvement in relations between the Roman authorities and the Yishuv: Caesar was sympathetic to all Jews within the empire, and regarded them as allies. At the very beginning of his war with Pompey, Caesar planned to dispatch Roman forces to the Land under the command of Aristobulus. And after his victory (in 48 B.C.E.) Hyrcanus and his adviser, Antipater the Idumean, went over to Caesar's side, and gave him vital support when he was besieged in Alexandria by Ptolemy XII, King of

---

[42] JIL, pp. 142-143
[43] JIL, p. 144

Egypt. Once he had overcome Ptolemy's army, Caesar proceeded to set the affairs of Judaea in order. Hyrcanus was confirmed in office as high priest and ethnarch, and the claims of Antigonus, son of Aristobulus, were rejected. The walls of Jerusalem, which had been destroyed by Pompey, were rebuilt, and the port of Jaffa was restored to Judaea." [44]

But the Ides of March, 44 BCE, brought ill to more than Caesar alone. His assassination plunged the whole Mediterranean world into war. The Parthians invaded Syria in 40 BCE.

"Antigonus the Hasmonean, who had been rejected by Caesar, seized the opportunity to ally himself with Rome's enemies and reclaim the throne of his fathers. The great majority of the Jewish nation supported Antigonus, who became king of Judaea, thus reviving the Hasmonean monarchy. As a counter-measure, the Roman generals Mark Antony and Octavian proclaimed Herod, the son of Antipater, as king." [45]

The Romans soon routed the Parthians and loosed their legions against Judaea. In 37 BCE, Jerusalem fell after a 5-month siege and Antigonus, the last of the Hasmonean kings, was executed. [46]

3.5.2 Herod "The Great"

Herod (37-4 BCE) was dominated completely by Rome, the norm with its vassals. Treated as an ally, "in fact, his hands were tied in every matter of political importance." Judaea was extended to most of the entire Land. Through iron rule and careful concessions, and foreign-laced forces, he kept the peace, his fame and status attracting visitors from throughout the Greek world.

Herod was Judaea's great builder. He built new cities – Caesarea on the ancient site of Strato's Tower, which became the country's largest port; Sebaste on Samaria; Herodian, southeast of Jerusalem – and added magnificence to Massada. "Jerusalem itself was transformed into one of the most splendid capitals of the east." He rebuilt the Temple, which became "Herod's Temple," and a royal palace, ampitheatre and great towers in Jerusalem. "But he never overcame public resentment of his submission to Roman ideology and control, exemplified by foreign atmosphere at his court and new Hellenistic towns and temples."[47]

---

[44] JIL, pp. 144-145

[45] JIL, p. 145

[46] JIL, p. 145

[47] JIL, pp. 146-147. On Herod's building activities, see also Parkes, pp.38-40.

3.5.3   The Great Revolt

On Herod's death, rebellions against his Roman-confirmed sons – Archelaus in Judea, Idumea and Samaria, and Herod Antipas in Galilee and Jewish Transjordan – were quickly suppressed. Archelaus proved too brutal even for Rome, which exiled him to Gaul, making his areas a province under a Roman-appointed official, the "procurator." This still "left the local Jewish institutions with a considerable measure of autonomy," especially the Sanhedrin, a court regarded by the Jews as "the principal ruling body in the nation," but really controlled by Rome through the procurators, some of whom, e.g., Pilate, exercised fuller control than others.[48]

Hoping to maintain calm, the Romans "took considerable pains at first to consider the religious feelings of the Jewish population," prohibiting statues and portraits in Jerusalem, but the Jews' hostility to Roman rule grew. Clashes occurred under Pilate, procurator from 26 to 36 CE, the most serious when Romans sought to hang banners bearing the emperor's portrait in Jerusalem. "The attempt aroused the entire nation, and Pilate gave way."[49]

A "really grave break" came in Emperor Caligula's (37-41 CE) reign, when the foreign minority in Yavneh set up an altar to him, which the Jews smashed. Caligula retaliated by ordering, among other provocations, erection of an "enormous golden image" in the Jerusalem Temple itself. An appeal by Agrippa I, Rome-educated grandson of Herod who had great influence in Rome and had been given the title of "king," achieved some relief, "but it was only the assassination of the emperor in 41 C.E. that prevented the outbreak of a Jewish-Roman war." Agrippa's close friend Claudius succeeded Caligula and made Agrippa "king of the entire Land of Israel." The popular Agrippa "worked tirelessly to strengthen and revitalize the Yishuv, and many regarded him as the heir of the Hasmoneans rather than the grandson of Herod. But after his death in 44 C.E., Judaea became a Roman province again, with all that this status involved." Twenty-two years passed between Agrippa's death and the Great Revolt, in which "Roman oppression grew ever more severe, clashes ever more frequent."[50]

---

[48] JIL, pp. 147-148
[49] JIL, p 148
[50] JIL, pp. 149-150

"Under Florus, the last procurator (64-66C.E.), the situation became impossible. Roman rule in Judaea was bankrupt; the official Jewish institutions, despite their autonomy, lost all prestige and influence. Anarchy developed, both in Jerusalem and in the countryside." [51]

In this era, the "Zealots" arose, religiously like the Pharisees, but regarding submission to foreign rule itself, even in the absence of a threat to Jewish survival, a grave religious transgression. This was the era too of the great Pharisee rabbis whose names have come down to us: Hillel, greatest sage of his generation and president of the Sanhedrin, and his grandson and Sanhedrin successor, Rabban Gamliel the Elder; Hillel's great rival Shammai, whose school seems to have associated with the most extreme zealots, and Shammai's distinguished associate, Rabban Yohannan Ben Zakkai. The Sadducees too were active, led by families that produced the high priests of the period, as were the Essenes, with their own Hasmonean period roots, whom Philo and Josephus recorded were to be found throughout Judaea, and Pliny recorded as having a settlement west of the Dead Sea.[52]

"By the end of the Second Temple period, the Jews formed a majority in the Land, though we have no definite figures. Most lived in Judaea, Galilee, and Transjordan, but there was a considerable number in the Hellenistic cities on the coast – cities like Ashkelon, Caesarea, and Acre. Idumea was completely Jewish, and the Jews predominated in north-west Samaria. The only area without a Jewish population loyal to the Temple in Jerusalem was the interior of Samaria, around Shechem, where the Samaritans, distinct in their religion and origin, continued to form a wedge between the Jews of the north and south. Though the majority of Jews lived in the villages, a number of the urban centers – Jerusalem, Jericho, Sepphoris, and Tiberias, for example – were entirely or largely Jewish." [53]

Jerusalem was among the world's famous cities, its Temple making it the Jewish world's hub. Highly prosperous Galilee, with many villages and towns and the Jewish cities of Sepphoris and Tiberias, was second in importance only to Jerusalem. "The outstanding characteristic of the Yishuv during this period was its fidelity to the Jewish faith, and in particular to the concept of monotheism as it had crystallized in previous generations." The old overt struggle with Hellenism was over. The foreign world influences were felt, but "there was no longer any deliberate pan-

---

[51] JIL, p. 150
[52] JIL, pp. 150-151
[53] JIL, p. 251

dering to foreign ideas." Literal willingness of the people to die rather than transgress the Torah, "an outstanding characteristic of Judaism" from the time of Antiochus Epiphanes, became "an historical factor of the first importance, for it largely determined the Roman authorities' attitude to the Jews."[54]

"Of all the institutions created by the Jews during the Second Temple period, it was the synagogue that had the greatest influence on the development of their culture: gradually it became the center of Jewish religious and public life. At the end of the period there were synagogues at Tiberias and Kfar Nahum (Capernaum); and in Jerusalem there were special synagogues for Jews from the Hellenistic Diaspora. The synagogue provided a unique setting for the worship of God – a worship freed from the bonds of elaborate and expensive ritual." [55]

The Great Revolt had multiple causes, including the mere presence of foreign rule to some Jews and the onerous Roman taxation to more. Rome favored the Hellenistic cities over the Jews with whom the Greek towns' citizens repeatedly clashed. Jews from all parts of the Land found cause to participate in the revolt.[56]

"Unlike the Hasmonean rebellion and the rebellion of Bar Kochba, the Great Revolt did not produce a central personality who could command the confidence of all. And the absence of a united leadership was a major obstacle to the effective deployment of Jewish forces at various stages of the revolt. Nevertheless, Judaea was the only eastern province to rebel on a large scale against the Roman Empire in that epoch." [57]

Clashes between Jews and the majority inhabitants in Caesarea, and the last procurator, Florus, confiscating large sums from the Temple, ignited the fury of the Yishuv; the Revolt was on. The Romans' local auxiliary forces were completely unable to handle it. The governor of Syria intervened at the head of his legions, and was routed in the hills of Judaea. The Jews' victory united the entire Yishuv under their banner. A provisional leadership was set up in Jerusalem. Commanders were sent to all districts (Joseph son of Mattathias, later known to the world as Josephus, to Galilee). "The Emperor Nero could not ignore the Jewish revolt. For in addition to imperiling the province of Judaea – the heart of an area vitally important to the empire – the rebels had disrupted Nero's

---

[54] JIL, p. 152
[55] JIL, p. 153-154
[56] JIL, p. 158
[57] JIL, p. 158

63

military plans for further conquests in the east. The governor of Syria's defeat compelled him to send additional legions to the Judaean front. The command of these legions was entrusted to Vespasian, one of the empire's most experienced generals."[58]

In 67 CE Vespasian's legions entered Galilee, where heroic defense under Josephus' command held them off for 47 days. But the fortress fell, and shortly the whole of western Galilee was in Roman hands. Jaffa, where the Jews were threatening Roman maritime transport and communications with Egypt, was next. "The city was taken by a Roman column, the Jewish ships were destroyed in a naval battle, and an occupation force was left in the city to control the neighboring towns and villages, which had large Jewish populations." Further victories over Jewish forces in the Golan and at Mount Tabor and Gush Halav completed Roman conquest of the north. Civil war erupted among the Jews and almost the whole of the country was occupied by the Romans. "Civil war in Rome held up further operations against Jerusalem, but at the beginning of July 69 C.E. Vespasian was crowned emperor by the legions in the east, and in the spring of the following year his eldest son Titus was able to lead the Roman forces against the capital." The rebel factions failed to unite, with fatal result.

"The fall of Antonia opened the way for a direct assault against the Temple Mount, and during the first half of the Hebrew month of Av (July-August) the Romans succeeded in overcoming its defenders. Titus ordered his troops to burn the Temple to the ground, intending by this action to destroy the main root of Jewish strength and inspiration. With the burning of the Temple, the Jews' last hope of victory vanished."[59]

"The stragglers fled to the Upper City," where Josephus recorded that Titus somberly addressed their last pockets of resistance: "Your people is dead, your sanctuary gone, your city is at my mercy."[60] But invaders whom the Yishuv in the end outlasted had pronounced the final doom of Israel before, starting with "Israel is laid waste, his seed is not!" almost thirteen hundred years earlier, and this time too the pronouncement – "Your people is dead" – proved premature. Despair must have overcome many, but within the hearts of some, e.g., the Jerusalem rabbi who obtained Roman

---

[58] JIL, p. 158

[59] JIL, pp. 158-161

[60] Quoted in Alon, p. 4

64

permission for a religious academy outside Jerusalem,[61] the Jewish heritage torch – already passed between a millennium's generations still in what we today call "ancient" history – burned on.

"Two roads led out of Jerusalem," the scholar Jacob Neusner wrote in *First Century Judaism In Crisis*, "one to Yavneh, the other to Massada." In stark terms, Neusner stated his view of the historic consequence of the choice made by those who trod each:

"Massada left behind a few fragments of cloth, some coins, smashed rocks and bones, a monument to futile, barren courage. Yavneh left behind twenty centuries of life, and, I think, many more to come."[62]

This book's next chapter follows the road of life that led through Yavneh. But those who trod that dead-end road to a desert mountain last stand left the Jewish people a more living legacy than a few fragments of cloth. JIL:

" . . . only a few isolated centers continued to hold out. The last of these was Massada, which was defended by the remnants of the rebels, under the command of Ele'azar Ben Ya'ir, until the year 73 C.E. The heroic death of Massada's defenders, who remained faithful to the principles of liberty and preferred to die by their own hands rather than fall into Roman captivity, provides a sublime and tragic epilogue to the Great Revolt."[63]

The most casual Jewish visitor who climbs Massada today, almost two millennia later, and stands amidst the Jewish ruins on the summit and gazes down on the remains of the Roman encampment and Roman siege ramp, just as detailed by Yadin in *Massada* and Vilnay in his incomparable *Guide* (pp. 321-328), and by Josephus almost two millennia earlier, connects not to a tragic epilogue but to a courage neither futile nor barren.

---

[61] Vilnay, p. 253, records laconically: "Tradition has it that when the Romans surrounded Jerusalem and its fall was imminent, Rabbi Yohanan, son of Zakkai, came before the Roman Commander and requested that the town of Yavne and the care of its sages be given over to him. This request was granted ...." I much prefer Max Dimont's description (*Jews, God and History,* pp. 107-109) of the rabbi springing out of a coffin before the astonished Vespasian, prophesying he'd soon be crowned Emperor and, if that came to be, requesting permission to start a small school of Jewish learning in some town in Judaea. The rabbi's prophesy came true and the request was granted. The academy was started in Yavneh. Dimont: "It was destined to play a central role in Jewish survival."

[62] Neusner, pp. 156-157
[63] JIL, pp. 158-161

65

3.5.4   The Bar-Kochba Revolt

The Tenth Legion set up camp in Jerusalem's ruins. Roman veterans were settled in the country. Non-Jewish cities were elevated in importance. Flavia Neapolis was founded in Samaria near Shechem. Tens of thousands of Jews had been killed in battle, tens of thousands taken captive. Large areas of land were confiscated. Newcomers were settled. Jews became tenants on land they had owned. Taxation was heavy. Jerusalem was depopulated.[64]

"Yavneh, predominantly Jewish even before the revolt, now became the spiritual and social center of the Yishuv and seat of Jewry's new leaders, Rabban Yohanan Ben Zakkai and Rabban Gamliel the Second." Judaea proved resilient. "There were important Jewish settlements at Emmaus, Gamzu, Gophna, and Jericho – in fact, in all the remaining towns and villages of what was formerly Judaea." Jews settled again in Caesarea, Acre and other non-Jewish coastal cities. The Temple's destruction created a spiritual vacuum, as the Romans had doubtless intended, but Ben Zakkai established a court and academy in Yavneh, and later Gamliel II made the court the supreme national authority.[65]

There was relative calm in the Land for sixty years. But then Hadrian decided to build on Jersualem's ruins a new city, Aelia Capitolina, with a temple honoring Jupiter. Confronted with this and other indignities, the Jews revolted again. "This time the revolt was carefully planned, under a single, determined leadership," but they faced Rome at the zenith of its power, able to unleash its best legions against them.[66] This 132 CE revolt was led by Shim'on Bar Kosiba – known as Bar Kochba –, supported by Ele'azar the priest and the great sages, led by Rabbi Akiva Ben Yosef. Evidenced by the words of the Romans' chroniclers themselves, Judaea's Jews fought ferociously. They captured Jerusalem and held it against the Tenth Legion and legions from Syria. JIL:

"Hadrian was forced to resort to extraordinary measures: legions were dispatched from various parts of the empire and placed under the command of Julius Severus, who was recalled from Britain. Uncertain of the size of the rebel army, but knowing its courage, Severus refrained from open combat, hoping to crush the rebels – as he did – by degrees. In the

---

[64] JIL, p. 161
[65] JIL, pp. 161-162
[66] JIL, p. 162

last stages of the revolt, the center of Jewish resistance was Beitar, south-west of Jerusalem, and it was there that Bar Kochba fell. Jewish losses were tremendous: Dio Cassius wrote of the destruction of 580,000 men. The Romans themselves suffered heavy casualties – so heavy, in fact, that in his report to the Senate, Hadrian omitted the customary formula: 'I and my army are well.'"[67]

Here indeed are Roman historian Dio Cassius' words, describing the final battles in ancient times of the Israelites who'd arrived or arisen in The Land a thousand four hundred years earlier:

"At first the Romans held them of no account. But when now the whole of Judea was disturbed, and the Jews everywhere in every land were likewise troubled and conspired with the rebels and wrought much hurt to the Romans, both in secret and openly (many others also of alien folk joining with them for the sake of gain), and the whole world was moved thereat, then at last Hadrian sent against them his best generals, of whom Julius Severus was foremost in command, being called from Britain of which he was governor.

"But Severus risked not giving open battle against the enemy in any place, seeing their numbers and their fury. Therefore, cutting them piecemeal by flying columns of greater strength under commanders of lower ranks, intercepting also and depriving them of supplies, he was able by this method, a slower one indeed, yet one less perilous, to wear them down and so to crush them utterly. Very few in fact survived. Of their forts the fifty strongest were razed to the ground. Fifty-eight myriads of men were slaughtered in skirmish and in battle. Of those who perished by famine and disease there is no one that can count the number.

"Thus the whole of Judea became desert, as indeed had been foretold to the Jews before the war. For the tomb of Solomon, whom these folk celebrate in their sacred rites, fell of its own accord into fragments, and wolves and hyenas, many in number, roamed howling through their cities.

"Many also of the Romans were slain in the war. Wherefore Hadrian, writing to the Senate, would not use the Emperor's wonted opening form of words, 'I and the army are well.' (Dio Cassius, Cocceianus, c. 155 - c. 235, Roman History, 1xix)."[68]

Near the end of JIL's chapter is a poignant photo of the view looking out from one of Bar Kochba's caves, the high wilderness hideouts of the last stages of the second revolt. The view looks to the east, at barren wilderness slopes between which one can glimpse a Dead Sea. It's a very different Promised Land view from the one Moses surveyed, looking west from the Jordan's opposite shore, a millennium and four centuries earlier.

---

[67] JIL, pp. 162-163
[68] Quoted in Tal, p. 127

Chapter 4
Romans, Christians, Jews

4.1 Evidence of Vibrant Jewish Presence in the Roman Era

So widespread is the misperception that the Romans exiled Judaea's Jews following the Great or at latest Bar Kochba Revolt[1] that an account of the Jews' post-revolt homeland history must begin by sampling the evidence that they remained in their homeland, and not as stray individuals but as the organized, self-aware, homeland-claiming Yishuv. Vilnay will be our principal guide.

4.1.1 Vibrant Urban and Rural Centers of Jewish Life

Caesarea: Important gentile city with large Jewish community, whose scholars are renowned in the Talmud. Vilnay, p 366. Jewish candelabra dated to 2nd - 4th centuries. Vilnay, p 371.

Akko: Important town, large Jewish community. Vilnay, p 397.

Haifa: 3rd century community noted in Talmud. Vilnay, p 381.

Tsipori [Sepphoris]: Largest, most important Galilee city in 1st-4th centuries CE, "great spiritual center," seat of renowned Hebrew academies and home of eminent Talmudic scholars. Mishnah edited, compiled here. Vilnay, pp 469-470.

Beit-She'arim: Seat of Sanhedrin in 2nd century. Destroyed c. 4th century. Uncovered remains include 2nd century synagogue

---

[1] E.g., Jimmy Carter, *Palestine: Peace Not Apartheid*, New York, Simon & Schuster, 2006, "Historical Chronology," p. 2: "135: Romans suppress a Jewish revolt, killing or forcing all most Jews of Judaea into exile."

destroyed by Romans in 352 as punishment for inhabitants' resistance to Roman rule, and among the largest Jewish catacombs in the land. Vilnay (pp 420-428) describes its facades, sarcophagi and inscriptions in great detail. 4th century olive press also found.

Tiberias and Galilee: Seat of great academies and famous sages after Jerusalem's fall. Jersualem (Palestinian) Talmud completed here c. 400 CE. Tombs of 1st-3rd century scholars, including Akiba (Vilnay pp 478, 484). 2nd-4th century Jewish inscriptions found in Kfar Kana (Vilnay p 473), Alma (Vilnay p 533) 2nd-3rd century Jewish monument in Rama (Vilnay p 543-544); amulet from 2nd-3rd century burial cave in Meona (Vilnay p 547).

Mishmar Ayelon: 2nd – 3rd century Jewish lamp, Vilnay, p 212.

Lod: Jewish academy in 2nd – 3rd centuries, Vilnay, p. 215.

Yavneh: 2nd century sages' academy. Vilnay, p 257. Mishnah begun here, completed in Galilee in 2nd century. Vilnay, p 253.

Ashkelon: 2nd – 3rd Jewish oil lamp, Vilnay, p. 266.

Ashdod: 2nd-3rd century marble slab, candelabrum, Vilnay pp 273-275.

Wilken, *The Land Called Holy* (pp 196-197): "[Jews avoided] the designation Palestine (which Christians freely used) as well as Greek and Roman names for cities and towns of Eretz Israel. In their view these names were ephemeral, without root, and, in the face of the eternity of Israel, would one day vanish."

See also Parkes (pp. 44-45), listing urban and rural communities, stating: "The population remained as it had been before the loss of independence, primarily peasants and landowners . . . . Jewish villages were thickly scattered in the hills and valleys of the region."

4.1.2 Synagogues as Evidence of Vibrant Jewish Life

Post-revolt synagogues furnish grassroots evidence that the Jews, as Jews, remained in the land. The synagogue that replaced the destroyed Temple, wrote Hershel Shanks in *Judaism In Stone: The Archeology of Ancient Synagogues* (Washington, Biblical Archeology Society, 1970), p. 12:

"was not a place for professional priests; it was a place for the people. Its Hebrew name, *beit Knesset,* as well as the Greek word synagogue, means house of assembly, a place where the people gather. Its focal ritual was not sacrifice, but the public reading of the Law and prayer."

Remains of Roman-Byzantine era synagogues, where ordinary Jews of the land communally expressed their Jewishness, abound.

The **Beit She'arim** synagogue, destroyed by Romans for 4th century Jewish resistance to Roman rule, "from the size of the remains" was "among the biggest in the country." Vilnay, p 420.

The famous synagogue in **Capernaum** (Kfar Nahum), extensively described by Vilnay (pp. 495-501), was once dated to the 2nd or 3rd century, but now thought to be later. See Alon, p. 29 and note.

In **Meiron**, site of many sages' tombs, is a 2nd century synagogue the façade of which is almost intact. Vilnay, pp. 536-537.

Vilnay shows a stone chair from the c. 3rd century synagogue of **Korazim**, in Galilee. Vilnay, pp. 103, 536-537. Wilken, *The Land Called Holy* (p 196), cited many synagogues in **Upper Galilee**, "a region that was populated largely by Jews and was slow to accept Christianity. In the course of the 4th and 5th centuries at least fifteen synagogues were constructed in the region, and many of these were no more than an hour's walk from each other."

Vilnay (p 102) shows "candelabrum from **Tiberias** carved in stone and found in the ruins of an ancient synagogue of the 3rd century."

Vilnay (p 228) shows in **Ashkelon** a "marble tablet carved with a candelabrum (menora), lulav (palm branch), shofar (trumpet) and ethrog (citron), 3rd century A.D."

At **Beit Yerah**, a 2nd century synagogue's remains. Vilnay, p 455.

In **Hammata,** 2nd-3rd century synagogue remains. Vilnay, p 486.

Vilnay pp 516,540-542: 2nd-3rd century **Kfar Biram** synagogue.

He shows religious objects from the 2nd – 3rd century synagogue at **Peki'in**, a many centuries old Galilean community claiming continuous Jewish presence since ancient times. Vilnay, p. 545.

He shows a carved stone found in **Hanita**, "probably the remains of a synagogue from the 2nd – 3rd centuries." Vilnay, p 551.

"The **Golan** is an integral part of the Land of Israel and of its history, as related in the Holy Scriptures. . . . Many ruins, also of synagogues of 2d-3d centuries, testify to its dense population in ancient times." Vilnay, pp. 552-553.

Beit Guvrin: "Jewish capital, carved with a candelabrum (menora) from an ancient [3rd century] synagogue," Vilnay, p 276.

"The Great Mosque, whose lofty tower can be espied from the distance, is located in the centre of the town [of **Gaza**]. It is built on the remains of a Crusader church of the thirteenth century dedicated to Saint John the Baptist. One of its pillars, the remnant of a 3rd century synagogue, is carved with a seven-branch candelabrum (menora) and a Hebrew and Greek inscription (fig.)." Vilnay, p. 300. See also Shanks, *Judaism In Stone*, pp. 35-36.

"... the Christian village of **Yafi'a** (Japhia of the Bible), one of the towns of the tribe of Zebulun ... was a stronghold of the Jews in their revolt against the Romans, in 66 AD. The Arabs call it Yafa. Remains of a synagogue ["3rd-4th centuries"] were discovered in the village. They are now covered up." Vilnay, pp. 456-457.

Beit Netofa: "ruins known in Arabic as Umm el-Amab – Mother of the pillars –, of which one is still standing. These are the remains of an ancient synagogue of the 3rd century" Vilnay, p 475.

"Relics of an ancient synagogue of the 3rd-4th centuries can be seen in the small valley to the east of **Gush Halav**," near Safad, Vilnay, pp. 539-540. Wilken, pp 195-196, cited the archeological record of two Gush Halav synagogues as showing that "the continuity of life over generations and centuries." Indeed, he understated what 300 years' evidence showed, repeated instant restoration of natural disaster damage evincing the tenacity of Jews' attachment. Wilkens' dates: "c 250 CE: constructed; 306: damaged by earthquake; 306: repaired; 362: again damaged by earthquake; 362: repaired; 447: damaged by third earthquake; 447: repaired; 551: damaged by massive earthquake, taken over by squatters."

Vilnay (p 102), 5th century synagogue mosaic in **Hulda**, 5th-6th century mosaic in **Jezreel** (p 106), 5th-6th century synagogue mosaic in **Jericho** (p 176), 5th century lead weight with candelabrum in **Ashdod** (pp.273-275), 5th-6th century synagogue remains in **Maon** (p 304), candelabrum in mosaic from 5th century synagogue in **Tirat Tsevi** (p 449), 6th century mosaic, probably from synagogue, in **Shiloh** (p 181), 6th century synagogue floor in **Beit Alpha**, "one of the most beautiful Jewish relics in the Holy Land" (pp 434-437), and 6th century synagogues in **Kunetra** (p 554) and **Hamat Gader** (p 555). Some of these and other 6th century synagogues are in Avi-Yonah (Avi2, pp 136-139,145-148), and still others of the Roman-Byzantine period in Wilken, pp. 194 ff.

71

Avi-Yonah further refers to a 4th century anti-Christian emperor's abortive attempt to rebuild the Temple, stopped by an earthquake and then by his death. "Even after this adversity, the Jews were able to maintain their status in the country, and shared in the material prosperity of the Byzantine period. The numerous synagogues of the 4th to 7th centuries attest to this." Avi2, pp. 137-141.

Wilken shed further light on these symbols of continued Jewish connection to the Land – Roman Emperor Julian's abortive effort to rebuild the Temple, and late Byzantine era synagogues:

"How Julian's proposal was greeted by Jews is unknown except from what is reported in Christian and pagan sources. According to these admittedly hostile accounts, 'The Jews were seized by a frenzied enthusiasm and sounded trumpets' when they heard of the plan. Some donated money for the building. Others claimed that 'one of their prophets had returned,' and they taunted Christians that their rule would be restored (Rufinus, h.e. 10.38). . . . Jews, said John Chrysostom, went about 'boasting that they would get back their city again.'"[2]

Avi-Yonah: "The Jews were able to maintain their status in the country, and shared in the material prosperity of the Byzantine period. The numerous synagogues of the 4th to 7th centuries attest to this."[3] Wilken:

"Jewish life in Palestine went on undisturbed during the Christian era – such is the testimony of archeology. The construction of new synagogues and the remodeling of older buildings continued without interruption. With few exceptions Jews were to go about their communal affairs and practice their way of life without interference. Jews also shared in the prosperity and economic growth that permeated the country as a whole, and Jewish intellectual life, as reflected in the Jerusalem Talmud and the midrashim, flourished."[4]

On vitality-evidencing evolving synagogue design and décor over the Roman-Byzantine era, see Avi2, pp. 107-121, 137-141.

4.1.3 Religious Achievements, Roman-Recognized Institutions

Beyond the archeological evidence of Jewish communities and synagogues as manifesting vibrant Jewish life in the land during the post-revolt Roman-Byzantine era, are two further evidence

---

[2] Wilken, p. 139
[3] Avi2, pp. 137-141
[4] Wilken, pp. 194-195

lines discussed below – great religious works, fragments of which have come down to us, and Roman recognition of the Patriarch as head of the homeland Jewish community until the 5th century.

4.2   Palestine: Still the Homeland of Jews

A further misperception, beyond that the Romans expelled the Jews, is that the Muslim Arabs called "The Palestinians" are Palestine's aboriginal natives. Non-Arab pagans, Christians and Jews were Palestinians first, and Jews have remained Palestinians still.

Canaan, Israel and Judah, Yehud and Judaea had been the Land's pre-Roman names. On destroying Judaea, Hadrian came up with "Palestine" – recalling the old Aegean "Sea People" Philistines, who'd long before "disappeared as a people under the heel of the Babylonians" – to replace the name of the country the Romans had called "Judaea" on coins they had minted themselves.[5] The Romans' intent in replacing "the historic name of the country" was to obliterate Judaea's historic Jewish identity.[6] But the name change didn't create a country called "Palestine." Parkes:

"...from the Arab conquest until the British Mandate it ["Palestine"] was never even a name on the political map of the world. It was a portion of some larger unit, whether Arab, Mamluk, or Turkish; and its people were never conscious of themselves as a national unit, nor did they ever attempt, as they had done in early and later Israelite days, to form an independent kingdom. During the long period of Islamic rule, with its kaleidoscopic changes of dynasty, no claimant to the throne of the caliphs, or even to a separate sovereignty, ever emerged from its population. It was the alternate prey of dynasties ruling from Damascus, Baghdad, Cairo or Istanbul ...."[7]

"Thus, up until the twentieth century, the name Palestine referred exclusively to the ancient land of the Jews – as did the names,

---

[5] "Further to commemorate the occasion [the 67-70 CE first defeat of the Jews] Titus struck coins on which Judah was represented by a woman sitting desolate under a palm tree, while around the coin was the melancholy inscription: 'Judaea devicta,' or 'Judaea capta.'" Abram Sacher, *A History of the Jews* (fifth ed.), p. 120. "In further commemoration of the great triumph Vespasian had the coins of that time inscribed with the words 'Judaea Capta,' 'Judaea has been taken.'" Solomon Grayzel, *A History of the Jews* (2d ed.), pp. 173-174. See also Heinrich Graetz, *History of the Jews* (JPS 1956 ed.), vol. 2, p. 314.

[6] Benjamin Netanyahu, *A Durable Peace: Israel and Its Place Among The Nations*, p. 4, quoting the historian Bernard Lewis.

[7] Parkes, p.11

Judea, Judah, Zion, and Israel. It never yet had been argued that there existed a "Palestinian people' other than the Jews."[8]

David Bar-Illan, late Editor of the *Jerusalem Post* and its "Eye On The Media" column, cited 20th century use of "Palestinian" to mean Palestine's Jews: "The Palestine Post (still the incorporated name of this newspaper), the Palestine Symphony, the United Palestine Appeal are typical examples." Also "The Anglo-Palestine Bank, The Palestine Electric Company, the Palestine Foundation Fund, the Palestine Philharmonic – the list is endless – were all Jewish institutions." He cited Arab aversion to using that name.[9] "Applying the term Palestinian to Arabs of Palestine probably began in the early 1960's, but neither Security Council resolution 242 of 1967 nor 338 of 1973 mentions Palestinians at all. It was only in the mid-Seventies that the term became popular."[10]

In 1992, Bar-Illan offered an explanation for the popularity of "Palestine" among Arabs following Israel's Six Day War victory. He began with the first article of the PLO Covenant, the core document of the Palestine Liberation Organization, founded to "liberate" Israel proper for "the Arab nation," written years before Israel held "occupied territories": "The people of Palestine is a part of the Arab nation." But, Bar-Illan continued, Arabs rightly concluded that an image of big, tough Israelis oppressing poor, helpless "Palestinians," as opposed to an image of a huge, hundreds-million strong "Arab nation" seeking vulnerable tiny Israel's obliteration, would garner stronger support in the West.[11]

Commence your inquiry into the lives of the Jews in the Land during its time known as Palestine with an understanding that it was with reference to long-gone Aegean Sea-people Philistines, not to today's Palestinian Arabs, that the Romans renamed Judaea to Palestine[12]; that they did so upon suppressing two ferocious revolts

---

[8] Netanyahu, *A Durable Peace: Israel and Its Place Among The Nations*, p. 4-5
[9] Bar-Illan, *Eye On The Media* compilation, pp. 166, 370, quoting Arab Prof. Philip Hitti testifying to the 1946 Anglo-American committee on Palestine: "There is no such thing as Palestine in history, absolutely not!"
[10] Bar-Illan, *Eye On The Media* compilation, p. 167
[11] Bar-Illan, *Eye On The Media* compilation, p. 370
[12] See article in Haaretz, 9/8/05, "Dig Backs Biblical Account of Philistine City of Gat": "Their [the Philistines'] best-known contribution was to the Roman name [hundreds of years after the Philistines' destruction by the Babylonians who

waged against them by armies of native Jews; and that prior to being ruled by Rome these native Jews had had their own fiercely Jewish Second Temple kingdom under the Hasmonean descendants of the Maccabees who'd wrested Judaean independence from the Seleucid heirs of Alexander the Great, who'd won the Land from the Persians who'd won it from the Babylonians and Assyrians, who'd won it from biblical kingdoms of Jews.

But the Jews, for all their tenacious, openly-Jewish, homeland-claiming presence in the land, were no longer its masters. Were they now living in "exile" in what had been their own land?

A 20th century scholar who addressed this question was Gedaliah Alon, author of *The Jews In Their Land In the Talmudic Age*. He made the case that the conquered Yishuv remained a homeland-residing people in Palestine, though in a deteriorating state, during the Talmudic Age, the era between the Revolts against Rome and the 7th century Muslim conquest of Palestine. (Alon added in an obiter dictum – a gratuitous comment outside the scope of the work in which it's included – that this homeland status subsequently came to an end, a dictum hotly contested in this book - jv)

And even Alon's assessment of a steadily fading brightness of Jewish life through the Roman-Byzantine era seems unwarranted in light of recent interpretations of both religious works and physical synagogue remains. Wilken, in *The Land Called Holy*, p. 195, quoting Levine, *Ancient Synagogues Revealed* (1982):

"Heretofore it has been commonly assumed that the late Roman-Byzantine period witnessed a steady decline of Jewish life and the recession into a kind of Dark Age which was to last for centuries. Large-scale emigration, loss of political status, lapse of key communal institutions, economic hardships and religious discrimination bordering at times on persecution, were assumed to have had their cumulative effect, leaving the Jewish community in an impoverished state. This perception has been challenged on a number of fronts. The Cairo Geniza has revealed a series of literary works dating from this period, including the existence of a creative cultural life among Jews. This impression is the result of the now-accepted dating to late antiquity of a series of liturgical, apocalyptic, halakhic, and mystical works, previously thought to be medieval in origin. To these examples can now be added the ever-increasing number of Byzantine synagogues being found throughout Israel. Moreover, other

---

finished of Judah] for the Land of Israel, 'Palestina,' which is derived from the Greek name 'Paleshet,' the land of the Philistines.' (There is no connection between the Philistines and modern Palestinians.)"

synagogues, products of a somewhat earlier age, continued to undergo extensive renovations, and were in use down to the Arab conquest of Palestine and beyond."

Alon applied to the Yishuv six tests of whether a foreign-conquered a people is still living in its homeland, and not "in exile": " a state of its own"; "a concentrated population making up a relative or absolute majority"; land ownership and a viable economic structure; its own leadership; "hegemony over any Diaspora that may exist"; and "if occupied, an active political stance[13] (including resistance and rebellion vis-à-vis the occupying power)."

Statehood

The State, "which had persisted in greater or lesser degree since the return from Babylon," was gone. "The Romans soon granted a form of national autonomy," but this was given to an "ethnos" living in Judaea. The Patriarch and Sanhedrin together provided only a "sociopolitical sort of leadership," not amounting to sovereignty. But Alon noted that the land was still called "Judea" until changed to "Syria Palaestina" by Hadrian after crushing the Bar Kochba revolt, and that even after that the name "Judea" persisted.[14]

Equivocal, perhaps, but see also Parkes, pp 45-46:

"The Roman recognition of a hereditary patriarchate in the House of Hillel was of the utmost importance for the Jewish community. It not only gave them a large measure of political autonomy in Palestine, but secured two other results. The Romans accepted the Patriarch as the supreme authority for the whole Jewish community within the empire, and so provided it with a religious as much as a political office, so that it retained in existence the theocratic conception of the Jewish people, and the intimate association between their political survival and religious loyalty."

Population

The Jews had suffered enormous losses through battle, starvation, deportation and persecution-induced emigration during the two revolts, "even after all this is taken into account, there are still no grounds for assuming that the Jews did not continue to form the majority of the inhabitants of Palestine," though banished from Jerusalem. His compiler footnoted: "Alon seems to imply a Jewish-Samaritan majority well into the 5th century at least."[15]

---

[13] Alon, p. 4
[14] Alon, p. 5
[15] Alon, pp. 5-6

Land Ownership and Economic Structure

Citing decrees by Vespasian and Hadrian divesting Jews of land title, Roman declarations declaring areas "judenrein," Jewish tradition recalling that Jews were reduced to tenant status on land they'd once owned, and a 4th century question posed in the Talmud – "Is most of the Land of Israel in Jewish hands or in Gentile hands?" – Alon concluded that there was a "constant deterioration." "And yet," he added, "in the final analysis, the sources at our disposal bear out the conclusion that no overwhelming decrease in Jewish land ownership in Palestine took place until near the very end of the [Talmudic, Romans-to-Arabs] period." He added that farming and processing farm products remained "the mainstay of the economic life of Palestinian Jewry throughout the period," and that there is "ample evidence" that the Yishuv also engaged in "a wide range of crafts, all of them productive."[16]

Leadership

Two central institutions, the Patriarch and the Sanhedrin, held the loyalty of the people, achieving first de facto and then de jure recognition by Rome. The Empire's adoption of Christianity led to the ending of the Patriarchate around 425 CE, but the Sanhedrin continued. Its authority diminished over time, "but this only strengthens our view that the entire period is one of transition, during which the image of a people living in its own country becomes blurred and faded, but is not obliterated."[17]

Hegemony Over Diaspora

Alon, acknowledging contrary views, held that the Patriarch's and Sanhedrin's authority over Diaspora Jews was not ad personam but, preserving a relationship dating back to the Second Commonwealth, was to institutions of the Homeland, not to religious leadership by happenstance in it. Through "legates" ("apostoloi"), the Patriachs could appoint and dismiss Jewish community leaders and exercise religious supervision abroad. The diaspora initially paid a tax to the Patriarch, and later supported the Palestine academies through a "levy of the Sages."[18]

---

[16] Alon, pp. 6-8
[17] Alon, pp. 8-10
[18] Alon, pp. 8-11

Alon acknowledged basis for belief that a "fairly balanced rivalry" for leadership existed between the Palestine and Babylonian communities from the 3rd through middle of the 4th centuries, with the latter then pushing Palestine "out of the picture," but he called this "untrue." "At no time up to the Moslem conquest did Babylonia capture the leadership." Instead, it remained "*subject to Palestinian authority* [emphasis original] up to the very end" of the Talmudic period. For this, Alon cited directional flow of correspondence showing Palestinians' higher authority settling disputed legal issues and questions of Jewish law and learning, the source of judicial appointments, and absence of Babylonian authority to impose monetary fines. "The relationship stands out most clearly in the well-known dependence of Babylonia on Palestine for determining the calendar." The Babylonian community had special status and a measure of independence greater than other diasporas, especially because of its Exilarchate of Davidic descent, but "one cannot deny that throughout our period Babylonia remained, like all the rest, under the effective authority of the Land of Israel."[19]

Political Resistance

Alon wrote that from the inception of Roman rule, Judaean Jews were unique in the Empire in their "rejection – even hatred – of Rome and her Empire." "Did this antipathy persist even after the Destruction? Of course it did." He contrasted Palestine Jews' agreement that Roman taxation was illegal (though many accepted "force majeure" need to pay it) with "the exact opposite" diaspora maxim in Babylonia that "the law of the sovereign is law for us."[20]

The Bar Kochba revolt, later insurrections in Sepphoris and elsewhere, and the Yishuv's "lively interest" in the Romans' and successor Byzantines' "relationships (and wars)" with Persia, and "the hopes they aroused for a possible turn in the fortunes of the Land of Israel," were to Alon evidence of "Palestinian Jewry's awareness of itself as a political force, capable of taking action."[21]

---

[19] Alon, pp. 10-12
[20] Alon, pp. 13-16
[21] Alon, p. 16

4.3 Periods of the Talmudic Era

So the Jews were still vibrantly communally there, still believing themselves the rightful owners of the Land, through Roman-Byzantine times. What was life like?

Alon divided the Talmudic Era, the five and a half century span from the Temple's destruction in 70 CE until the Arab conquest in 636, into three historical periods: from the destruction to the 235 end of the Severan Caesars' rule; from 235 to the Patriarchate's abolition in 420; and from 420 to the 636 Battle of Yarmuk.

4.3.1 "Time of the Tannaim" (70 – 235 CE)

In the wake of destruction of its political and religious institutions, self-definition and leadership struggles consumed the Yishuv.

Multiple parties strove for religious leadership in the post-Temple era – the priests, who'd had supplementary extra-Temple roles; the upper class, most inclined to cooperate with Rome; the Sages, internally divided in political view; and the Pharisees, "this band of teachers," by now composed of all walks of life, thanks to their program of public Torah study, through which they had forged close affection and discipline bonds with the mass of the people.[22]

The Patriarchate, originally embodied in the presiding officer of the High Court and head of the Academy, increasingly gained in these powers at the Sanhedrin's expense, and put itself forward "as spokesman for the nation vis-à-vis the Roman government."[23]

Another Yishuv self-defining task was "religious consolidation." In Temple times, Judaism could afford the "sometimes wildly differing schools of thought" of a multiplicity of religious sects.[24]

---

[22] Alon, pp. 21-24

[23] Alon, pp 24-25

[24] Recent decades' analyses, including of the Dead Sea Scrolls, have made late Second Temple Judaism seem even more diversified than scholars had formerly believed. Hershel Shanks, in *The Dead Sea Scrolls After Forty Years*, Biblical Archeology Society, Washington (1991), pp. 15-16: "The picture we get from the Qumran documents is of a much more varied Judaism before the Roman destruction than we had ever imagined. It is almost inaccurate to talk about Judaism. Many scholars talk about Judaisms." There are implications for Christianity too. Shanks continued: "We find not only a dedication to law but to messianism, apocalypticism, the end of days, mysticism, a whole range of beliefs, dualism. Many of these ideas we thought Christianty took from later Hellenistic sources,

But with the Temple gone, national survival was at risk. Spiritual-religious unification set in on the catastrophe's heels. "The end of the Temple sounded the death-knell of the Sadducees, and they vanished from the stage of Jewish history." Leaders declared "Jewish" Christians" to be "outside the community of Israel."[25]

Social consolidation paralleled the religious one. "Distinctions derived from family origin" began deteriorating on the Temple's destruction, and "the social situation in later tannaitic times practically wiped out such distinctions, thus curing the nation of a serious social defect." The distinctions of the priesthood (kohanim) gradually faded, and they merged into the mass of plain Jews. Some elements of dubious Jewishness were merged definitively into the community, but some were definitively excluded.[26]

"But the most distinguishing characteristic of this time-span [70-235] is the creation of a halakhic literature, fashioned out of that long chain of tradition known as the Oral Torah. The classic achievement is, of course, the Mishnah – the book which embodies the complicated process whereby the thinking of the nation about halakhah and law had been crystallized over the years. In its turn, the book was destined to serve as the basis for Jewish life and thought for many generations, in the homeland and in the Diaspora. During the next two or three centuries it became the foundation on which were erected those all-embracing structures which we know as the Talmudim – the Jerusalem Talmud and the Babylonian Talmud. But that was to come. It is the Mishnah which here engages our attention."[27]

"This age of the Mishnah" saw the Talmudic Age's highest official recognition of the Yishuv by its Roman overlords:

"It was the time when, externally, Roman recognition of the Patriarch as supreme leader of the Jews reached its peak; and the same goes for Jewish acceptance of his authority. This may very well be connected with the economic upswing during the reigns of Antoninus Pius and the Severan emperors (138-235). Additional evidence of this prosperity has been provided by archeological finds, especially in Palestine, where a number of beautiful synagogues built at the end of the second century and the beginning of the third, such as the one at Capernaum, have been uncovered."[28]

---

outside Palestine. Now we know that there were sources right in Palestine from which they could have been absorbed into Christianity."

[25] Alon, pp 25-26
[26] Alon, pp 26-27
[27] Alon, pp 27-28
[28] Alon, p 29

4.3.2 "Age of the Amoraim" (235 – 420)

A "half-century of turmoil," from which the Roman Empire "never really recovered," followed the Severan emperors' reign, "marked by foreign wars on the eastern and western marches of the Empire, and by bloody internal struggles between rivals for the throne of the Caesars."[29] None of Rome's provinces prospered. Alon: "There are grounds for assuming that at this time there was a drastic reduction in land-ownership by Jews; and that gentiles from outside the country acquired tracts of major proportions."[30]

Alon here introduced Arabs into Palestine's neighboring regions, and as marauders in Palestine.

"Any evaluation of this period must also take account of the fact that it witnessed the first penetration into Palestine of Arabs, who came as marauding nomads. Explicit evidence for this is provided by Christian literature dating from this time. However, even earlier Jewish sources going back to the middle of the third century apparently refer to the same thing when they speak of 'Sabaeans' breaking into a town, or mention armed brigands surrounding a town or a village.

"Such raids occurred more and more often in the fifth and sixth centuries. They brought in their train another development: permanent Arab settlements that took root in territories adjacent to Palestine, and showed signs of becoming a political factor in Palestine, itself. Here we have the beginning of the "Kingdom of Ishmael" mentioned in midrashim prior to the Muslim conquest. Indeed, these Arab settlements paved the way for that conquest, which gave the coup de grace [not so – jv] to the already weakened Jewry of Palestine."[31]

But factors "which enabled the Jewish people to survive in Palestine for as long as it did" were pilgrims and immigrants from the diaspora, and "annual contributions received by the Patriarch and the Sanhedrin from Jewish communities all over the world."[32]

"The cultural achievement of this second stage is best summed up by the monumental work which marks its close: the Jerusalem (or Palestinian)Talmud. Like the Mishnah, which marked the close of the first stage, the Yerushalmi too is the distillation of generations-worth of complex spiritual and cultural activity. Like the Mishnah, it too represents but a fraction of the halakhic creativity and interpretive study of the age whose landmark it is. The Amoraim carried on from where the Tannaim had left off, and

---

[29] Alon, p. 29
[30] Alon, pp 29-31
[31] Alon, p 32
[32] Alon, p 32

81

created many "Talmuds" based on the Mishnah. Only one such Palestinian Talmud has come down to us; but it is ample testimony to the spiritual
resources of a people whose creativity did not slacken or dry up even at a
time when the very foundations of society at large were crumbling."[33]

Alon's Talmudic Age's Stage II saw the Roman Empire's break
up, on the death of Emperor Theodosius in 395, into Western, with
it capital in Rome, and Eastern, with its capital in Constantinople.
Stage II's last quarter century occurred after this breakup.[34]

4.3.3   Byzantine Palestine (420 – 640)

Of the Talmudic era's six centuries, we know least of the final
two, and the picture of Palestine Jewry presented by even the
growing evidence we do now have remains murky.

The Emperor dismissed Gamliel VI, the last Patriarch, in office
since 400, in 425, ostensibly for violating a new synagogues ban.
If so, it was a defiant assertion by the Yishuv of its rights. But the
Patriarchate was gone. Its loss "must have gravely weakened the
central leadership of the nation. The aura of regality, the sense of
some surviving national dignity which had persisted as long as the
princely office was in existence ... had now vanished.... Nevertheless, some measure of central leadership remained."[35]

The Sanhedra'ot continued, especially in Tiberias, "where the
chief Sanhedrin had had its seat from the middle of the third century," and now "continued to be an active center of Jewish leadership for the country as a whole and for the Diaspora" throughout
these final two centuries. Alon added that despite the Empire's
decree that the "taxes" the Diaspora had annually paid to the Patriarchs be paid to the public exchequer, Diaspora Jews still managed
to support the Land's Jewish institutions such as the Sanhedra'ot.[36]

"This brings us," Alon continued, "to the question of population,"
the composition of which is uncertain. Alon wrote that "from the
4th century onwards the Christian presence in Palestine becomes
more noticeable," mostly from resident pagans' conversions. He
apparently believed Christians became a majority in the 6th century, with Jews at that time "over one-fourth of the total," an as-

---

[33] Alon, p 34
[34] Alon, p. 34
[35] Alon, p. 35. See also Alon, p. 739.
[36] Alon, p 35

sessment which his own editor contrasted with Avi-Yonah's in *The Jews of Palestine* that in the 5th century "a Christian majority was being created in Palestine for the first time in history."[37]

Parkes, p. 47:

"In the 4th century it is probable that Jews still formed a majority of the population of Galilee, but only a minority in the south where they had not recovered from the losses of 135. We cannot establish the fact statistically, but several Christian writers of the period, especially Jerome who lived in Bethlehem, reported that there were few Christians and that most of the people in the country were Jews. This evidence might have appeared conclusive, did we not know how easily men magnify numbers when stating that a district is full of people they dislike!"

Finally, Alon turned to "Jewish spiritual creativity" in this final phase of the Talmudic era. He judged it as largely based on sages' teachings going back "two or three generations and more." Still, he went on, "the gathering and editing of this literature, so that it was preserved for future generations, is the hallmark of the difficult years we are now describing." There was new creativity too:

"For this was the time when *piyyut* – the unique liturgical poetry of the synagogue – made its first appearance. In the *piyyutim* of Yannai, from all indications composed in the Land of Israel at the end of the Byzantine period, we discover this wonderful new literary genre already in full flower, combining halakhah, aggadah, prayer and art. It was to flourish for generations to come in many and varied forms, becoming a significant element in the bloodstream of Jewish life."[38]

Alon concluded with this commentary upon the linkage of its final centuries' spiritual creativity with both past and future:

"This phenomenon [piyyut liturgical poetry] too must have had antecedents. It could scarcely have sprung up full-grown, a sudden revelation of the sixth century. It probably grew out of that prayer-poetry – possibly also secular songs – of which there is some evidence from the days of Tannaim and Amoraim. Its ancestry may even go back to the poetic arts of the Second Commonwealth. Still, piyyut as piyyut did not appear on the scene until the end of our period. That was when it acquired the forms that were to characterize it for centuries to come: that was when it became an inalienable part of the Jewish heritage. It was as though a great period of Jewish history, about to move into the shadows, bequeathed a special legacy of its own to the generations that were to follow."[39]

---

[37] See Alon, p 36 and note 10.
[38] Alon, p 37
[39] Alon, pp 37-38

83

Chapter 5
Christians, Persians, Christians, Arabs, Turks

5.1 Christians, Persians, Christians

5.1.1 Christians

When the 614 CE Persians invaded, Jews had been living in the Land for one thousand eight hundred years, having arrived or arisen there in the Late Bronze/Iron I Age transition. Neighboring kings had written in stone of the "House of Omri" and "House of David." Later those Jewish kingdoms had stood and fallen to mighty empires of the early first millennium BCE.

Those Jews, whose Jerusalem kingdom had fallen in 586 BCE, twelve hundred years to the year before the Persians of 614 CE set foot in Jerusalem, had remained as "Yehud" under the 614 Persians' ancestors, and then as Judaea, taking on Alexander's successors and finally Rome. In words of Dio Cassius and Josephus, committed to parchment, and words and pictures – "Judaea Capta" and Temple plunder carved on the Arch of Titus in Rome – to metal and stone, mighty Rome had acknowledged to history that it had been from indigenous Jewish defenders, not a foreign conqueror, that it had wrested rule the land known to it as "Judaea."

Devastated, utterly decimated in two ferocious wars that had left not even the mighty Roman army well, still the Jews had remained on the land through ensuing centuries as the organized, vibrantly Jewish, homeland-claiming Yishuv, while the Roman Empire, which had sought to build a temple to Jupiter on the site of Solomon's Temple, split into two and officially adopted a new religion centered upon the resurrection of a Roman-crucified Judaean Jew.

And so Judaea's Jews were consciously communally there when the 614 Persians arrived to take on the Romans' Byzantine heirs.

5.1.2 Persians

The Jews, acting consciously in their ethnic and national interest, aided the Persians. "The alliance [sic] between Persia and the Yishuv was planned ahead by the Persian king, Khosrau II."[1] Galilee Jews "joined with the Persian invaders, helped in conquering Acre and participated in the successful siege of Jerusalem."[2] 20,000 to 26,000 fighters[3] came from Jewish communities in Galilee, the south of Palestine and Cyprus.[4]

"The mass participation of Jews in the war indicates that the Yishuv was large at the time, though it is impossible to gauge what percentage of the overall population was Jewish."[5]

The Jews believed they were fighting for an independent Judea, "still fighting for independence."[6] Their "considerable" military and other help to the invaders evidenced "Palestinian Jewry's awareness of itself as a political force, capable of taking action."[7]

The Persians had "promised the Jews self-government in Palestine within the framework of the Persian Empire, the rebuilding of Jerusalem as a Jewish city, and the restoration of the Temple."[8] They ruled Palestine from 614 through 628,[9] initially honoring their promises to the Yishuv. Dinur: "For three years, the Jews were apparently in full control of Jerusalem: recalcitrant Christians were held firmly in check, many apostates were sentenced to death as idolaters, and materials were gathered for the rebuilding of the

---

[1] JIL, p. 198. Avi-Yonah wrote that the Jews helped by a "revolt." Avi2, pp. 148-149.

[2] Bahat, p. 23

[3] Parkes, p 60; Peters, p 148, 153; Tal, p 127.

[4] DeHaas, p. 115.

[5] JIL, p. 198

[6] DeHaas, p. 115; Netanyahu, p. 26.

[7] Alon, p 16

[8] JIL, p 198

[9] DeHaas, p. 117

Temple."[10] Bahat in *The Forgotten Generations* shows a painted menorah on a building adjacent the Temple Mount made during this Persian-permitted attempt to rebuild the Temple.[11] Tal agreed that the Persian king "expressed his gratitude by giving the Jews permission to rebuild the Temple."[12]

This time it was Christians, strikingly lacking in rachmonas for Jews' 9th of Av lamentations, who were devastated by the Persians' seizure of Jerusalem from them. Wilken, pp. 217-218: "Nothing exemplifies better the transformation that had taken place in the Land of Israel than the obvious, yet seldom observed, fact that when Jerusalem was captured by the Persians in the seventh century of the common era, it was the Christians, not the Jews, who sang a lamentation over the Holy City."

How vastly different that 7th century Christian attitude toward Jerusalem seems from that of those Christians today who stridently campaign for Jerusalem's heart with its most holy of Christian and Jewish holy places to be taken from Israel and handed to a never previously existing Arab "Palestine" that will be part of the billion-plus world of vastly less secular Muslims. Maybe many such Christians under-appreciate their Western Christian civilization's post-biblical Palestine's heritage. Wilken (p. xii):

"Though in other ways they may be well informed about the Middle East, few realize that Christianity's role in the land of the Bible is not restricted to the time of Jesus and Christian origins. The Christian religion has a long history in Palestine, the history of indigenous communities whose fortunes have been linked to the many conquerors – Romans, Arabs, crusaders, Turks, and Jews – and of national communities from other parts of the world, Copts from Egypt, Armenians, Syrians, Ethiopians, Russians, some of which have uninterrupted histories from antiquity to the present."

They under-appreciate too Palestine's heritage, as distinct from Iraq's and Arabia's. Wilken (p. 23) wrote that with the coming of Alexander, "Palestine was joined to the West, first through the Hellenistic kingdoms of the Ptolemies and Seleucids, later through the Romans.... The people of Palestine became part of our history, the history of Greece and Rome and of Christianity, not simply a distant chapter in the fortunes of the ancient Near East."

---

[10] JIL, p 198. See also Katz, p 89.
[11] Bahat, pp 23-24
[12] Tal, p 31

5.1.3 Christians

Dinur put succinctly: "Persia's pact with the Yishuv was short-lived." It gave Palestine back to the Byzantine Christians, but even before that had utterly betrayed its erstwhile ally, the Yishuv.

"Persia's pact with the Yishuv was short-lived. The conquerors came to terms with the local Christians, a bishop was appointed to govern Jerusalem, and the Jews were expelled once again. Though there is no detailed historical record of events and their causes during the 14 years of Persian rule, it would seem that the Persians' shameless betrayal of the Yishuv impelled the Jews, especially the wealthy ones, to side with Heraclius, the Roman emperor."[13]

Among those wealthy Jews was Benjamin in Tiberias, with whom Heraclius stayed for a while. The Jews sent deputations to him there, receiving undying assurances yielding dying results:

"The emperor gave his word that the Jews would not suffer with the reinstatement of Roman authority. He signed a solemn contract, a written guarantee of Jewish safety — and almost immediately dishonored it when the Christians of Jerusalem and Galilee, arguing that the very existence of the Jews there placed them in grave danger, and the Jews would certainly side with any enemy that attacked the Christians, as they had with Persia. The Christians promised that a fast would be observed to atone for the imperial breach of faith. Heraclius gave way, and we are told that he killed every Jew he could find in the vicinity of Jerusalem and Galilee; many hid, or fled to the desert and the hills, or across the frontiers."[14]

Christians took revenge on Jews,[15] massacred Jews,[16] seriously diminishing Palestine Jewry for several centuries.[17] Vengeful persecution occurred.[18] Benjamin of Tiberias accepted Christianity.[19]

But the Jews were still there, ready to assist the next autonomy-promising invader, a few years later when the Arabs arrived.

5.2   Arabs, Turks

Dinur divided Palestine history from the Arab invasion to the Crusades into four time frames he called "the conquest, and the first occupation up to 660; the Mu-awiyyad [Omayyad] dynasty, 660-

---

[13] JIL, p 198
[14] JIL, pp 198-199
[15] Parkes, p 61
[16] Peters, p 148
[17] DeHaas. Pp 119-120
[18] Katz, p 89
[19] JIL, pp 198-199

750; the Abbassid dynasty, 750-969; and the Fatimid dynasty from 969."[20] This four-part period began with Arab invasion and rule, but it became before long a rule Arabs no longer ruled.

5.2.1 Conquest to 660

Parkes listed places supporting his statement that Palestine's Jews at the Arab conquest lived in all parts of the country, on both sides of the Jordan. Tiberias was their center, and they had begun to return to Jerusalem, though the Christians wanted them kept out.[21]

The Arabs who conquered Jerusalem in 640 ruled from Arabia,[22] but the great Muslim prophet Muhammed never entered Jerusalem. He had died in 632, six years before Jerusalem fell in 638 to the Arabs under Caliph Omar.[23] The surrender document was signed by Omar and the Patriarch Sophronius.[24]

The Jews, "who regarded the Islamic conquest and the replacement of the Byzantine-Christian rule by the Arab one as the beginning of the redemption of Israel,"[25] provided help once again to these latest invaders. "Settlement in Jerusalem resumed and the Jews were appointed guardians of the Temple Mount in return for their aid to the conquering army."[26] The Jews were rewarded in Hebron for aiding the Muslims by being allowed to rebuild their synagogue in front of the entrance to the Cave of Machpelah.[27]

Some lands taken from the Jews by Heraclius were returned. Dinur: "The owner could sell his land to a co-religionist, but not to a Muslim. The early caliphs were careful to preserve the [tax] system and to prevent Muslims from becoming land owners."[28]

---

[20] JIL, p 199

[21] Parkes, pp 72-73

[22] Parkes, p 64

[23] Tal, pp 61-62

[24] Tal, p 128

[25] Tal, p 65

[26] Bahat, p 23. Bahat's book (p 24) has a photo of a letter documenting an Omar-Sophronius debate. Omar, "wishing to repay the Jews for their help in the Moslem conquest of Palestine, demanded that 200 families be permitted to inhabit the town." Sophronius, "Patriarch and leader of the surrendered Christian community of Jerusalem," refused "obstinately." Omar settled for 70.

[27] Bahat, pp 24-25

[28] JIL p 202. Non-Muslim paid poll and land tax. Tal (p 102) cited Mjuir al-Din's 8th century history: "From the time of Caliph Abd-el-Malik (d. 705) and hence-

Parkes was firm that during the century after the Arab conquest, the land had "almost entirely" Christian and Jewish subjects. Then there were rich Arab landlords, "but this change of owners did not involve any extensive change in the nature of the population. The land still was worked by the same peasants, for the Arabs were not only entirely inexperienced in agriculture but heartily despised the tiller of the soil." For at least the next 100 years, the population was majority Christian, minority Jew and Samaritan.[29] Other historians agree. DeHaas wrote that Palestine's population in the 600's was an Arabic-speaking non-Arab mix.[30] Peters, citing Parkes, Hogarth, Hitti and Lewis: "During the first century after the Arab conquest, the Caliph and governors of Syria and The Land ruled almost entirely over Christian and Jewish subjects."[31]

The Muslim armies brought with them an intensity of religious fervor not seen since maybe the armies of Joshua. And for the first time all three world religions which have wrestled over the "Holy Land" ever since came face-to-face with both others.

When the Muslims captured Jerusalem in 638, the Temple Mount had been a holy site, The Holy Site, for Palestine's still present Yishuv for over one thousand six hundred years – from the time of King David. In that very century, sixteen centuries after King David, the Jews, acting under the express if brief leave of the then-current conqueror, had made yet one more attempt to rebuild their Temple on that same site still universally recognized – in reverence or ridicule – as the site of their Temple.

The invading Arabs, whose new Muslim faith had embraced the Biblical prophets from Abraham through Moses to Jesus, appreciated full well the significance to them, as well as to Christians and

---

forth Jews were among those who guarded the walls of the Dome of the Rock. In return they were absolved from paying the polltax imposed on all non-Moslems."

[29] Parkes, pp 66-68

[30] DeHaas, p 138. That Palestine's non-Arab inhabitants began speaking Arabic does not signify a greater "Arabization" of Palestine than of other pieces of the Muslim empire. Prof. Dinur (JIL, p. 199): "The assimilation of Palestine into the Arab world was vital to the general development of the Islamic Empire, which covered a great landmass from Spain and the Atlantic Ocean to LakeAral and Khorasan (in northeast Iran), from southern France and Sicily to the borders of-India and the Sunda Isles. Arabic became the common language of all these countries."

[31] Peters, p. 151; Parkes, p. 66.

Jews, of the holy sites in Jerusalem. Jerusalem had even been briefly, not by random selection, the Muslims' own first direction of prayer. Muhammad had acknowledged the concepts of 'the Promised Land' and 'the Chosen People' relating to the Jews.[32]

Clouded in detail-differing legends is the Omar-Sophronius encounter preceding the Arab conqueror's building of the first Muslim house of prayer where the Jewish Temple had stood. But "underneath," as Colin Thubron wrote in *Jerusalem*, the "truths" regarding immediate Muslim recognition of the reverence due the site "are there in harder shapes." In each version, Omar asks Sophronius to show him the site of Solomon's Temple and eventually arrives at the refuse-strewn Temple Mount, the sanctity of which Omar acknowledges by personally removing the debris Christians had heaped on it in deliberate disrespect for the Jews.[33]

---

[32] Tal, pp. 67-68, quoting the Encyclopedia Britannica (1971 ed, p. 641). Tal also quoted passages of the Koran showing that Muhammed "acknowledged the biblical concepts of 'The Promised Land' and the 'Chosen People' relating to the Jews." Ibid. See also Parkes (p. 167): "In the earliest days of his preaching, when the contrast between the lofty monotheistic Judaism and Christianity and the primitive paganism of Arabia was still vividly impressed on his mind, Muhammad showed his preference for these older faiths by making Jerusalem the city towards which his followers should turn in prayrer. But when it became obvious to him that neither Jews nor Christians were willing to accept his claims to a divine mission, entitling him to the position of the last and final authority on the revelation of God to man, he changed his mind."

[33] In Thubron's (pp 188-190) version of the Omar-Sophronius tale, Omar asked to be taken "to the site of the Temple of Solomon, and Sophronius, fearing that he meant to rebuild it, took him instead to the Church of the Holy Sepulchre," and thence to other churches, until Omar chanced upon the filth and refuse-inundated Temple site, which "Christians, angry with the Jews for inciting the Persian invasion of 614," had defiled in revenge. "With his own hands the caliph lifted the dung from the summit and hurled it into the Kidron valley, and a wooden mosque was built alone on the terraces." "All this may be legend," Thubron went on, "yet underneath, like ruins gilded over by the earth, the truths are there in harder shapes, and certainly Omar permitted the Jews, exiled by Heraclius, to return to the city; and from their earliest days the Moslems honored the rock," with its legends of Abraham and Jacob, on the site of Solomon's Temple.

DeHaas' (p 133) version is similar. Omar "asked to be taken to the Temple. Sophronius directed his steps to the Church of the Holy Sepulchre. Omar denied it was the Temple.... Explaining what he sought, he was told that the Sacred Rock would only be reached by crawling through the city sewer, and by wading through a water conduit. Crawling on hands and knees, the Caliph went through the sewer till he emerged on a high level space atop of a hill encumbered with

90

"The construction of the Dome of the Rock and the Mosque of Al-Aqsa on the very site of the Jewish Temple was a political move," Tal states, "designed to secure Muslim hegemony over any subsequent Jewish or even Christian claims. The Temple Mount was thus effectively sealed off from incursions, physical or spiritual, by other religions."[34] Omar built a small mosque on the site.[35]

"It was only 50 years later, that the Umayyad Caliph Abd-al-Malik built the magnificent Dome of the Rock (CE 692) — erroneously called the Mosque of Omar — on the same site, to commemorate the place of Abraham's sacrifice and Noah's Ark."[36]

"Caliph al-Malik wished to rebuild the Temple of Solomon."[37]

Historians have parsed the commonplace that "Jerusalem is holy to followers of three faiths: Muslims, Christians and Jews." Muhammed died in 632, six years preceding the Muslim capture of Jerusalem. Thubron summarized Muhammad's link to Jerusalem:

"Moslems say that Mahomet flew from Mecca on his mare, el-Burak, and alighted upon the hill's summit. The Koran declares 'Glory be to Him who carried His servant by night from the Sacred Mosque to the Faraway

---

ruins. Surveying the scene, he identified it as confirming Mohammed's report.... He scooped up the filth, and carried it away in his robe. In this act he was warmly imitated by his officers.... the ordure was removed to the neighboring valley, outside the city, and the sacred site purified and sanctified. Around this rock Omar built his mosque, the Mosque of Omar, which later gave way to its celebrated successor, the present Dome of the Rock." See also Avi-Yonah's similar account: "Leaving the Church of the Holy Sepulchre untouched, he [Omar] proceeded to the Temple esplanade and himself began to carry away the accumulated rubbish, with the assistance of the patriarch Sophronius." Avi2, p. 152. The Dome of the Rock, completed in 691, "is the earliest monument of Muslim architecture still standing." Avi2, p. 152.

Muslim accounts of the Omar-Sophronius encounter are very clear that Omar's siting of the first Jerusalem mosque on the site of Jews' Temple Mount was not mere historical happenstance. Prof. Wilken (p 238): "As in the Christian chronicles, the Temple Mount is pictured as being covered with a dung heap, and Umar expresses a desire to build a mosque in the city; but he does not engage in an aimless quest for the proper site to build the mosque. He knows exactly where he wanted the building to stand – on the site of the Temple of Solomon, which had been destroyed by Bukhnassar, the biblical Nebuchadnezzar. Accordingly, when Umar meets with the patriarch, after signing the 'treaty of capitulation,' he says to him, 'Take us to the sanctuary of David.'"

[34] Tal, p 31
[35] Tal, p 62
[36] Tal, p 62
[37] Tal, p 65

Mosque,' and although in mystic interpretation the 'Faraway Mosque' is-God Himself, popular imagination conceived it to be the Temple of Jerusalem, the most distant point of Moslem pilgrimage."[38]

David and his long line had dwelt in Jerusalem, indelibly branding upon it "City of David." Jesus had prayed, preached, suffered and died in Jerusalem. These are hard historical facts, not Jewish and Christian faith-based beliefs. Parkes dealt with "difficulty" from the historian's viewpoint of attributing Muslim sanctity to this site not coincidentally already sanctified on hard fact by others:[39]

"The difficulty of the historian is still further emphasized by the fact that the nature of the ascension of Muhammad is such that it is entirely useless as historical evidence. The association of Jews with The Land is a historical fact, whether one believes that association to be the result of a divine decision or not. The association of the Founder of Christianity with Galilee and Judea is a historical fact, whether one accepts the Christian theological claim as to His nature, or even the ecclesiastical claim of authenticity for the Holy Places. But the association of Muhammad with the country rests on willingness to believe that in a single night, and on a winged horse, Muhammad flew to and from Arabia in order that he might then mount by a ladder for a personal view of the heavens; that while his remarkable mount, al-Burak, remained tied near to that point in the whole area which stood above the only remaining Jewish Holy Place, the Wailing Wall. The event is not the poetical ortheological dramatization of an incident which, stripped of the miraculous element, rests on solid historical foundations. It has to be accepted as it stands, or there remains no evidence whatever associating Muhammad with Jerusalem other than the early choice and quick rejection of that city as the direction towards which Muslims should pray; and this choice, in any case, rested on a veneration for Judaism and Christianity and not on a personal experience of Muhammad."[40]

Parkes applied the same reasoning to the Land as a whole:

"What is true of Jerusalem turns out also to be true of the other sites in the country on the basis of which the claim is made that Palestine is the

---

[38]   Thubron, pp 188-190

[39]   Parkes, p 167

[40] Parkes, p. 168. See also Tal (pp. 66-67), quoting Prof. Werblowsky's *Meaning of Jerusalem to Jews, Christians and Moslems*, contrasting Christianity's and Islam's relationships of physical and religious facts: "Whereas in the case of Christianity the life and death of Jesus created religious facts (e.g., the resurrection and ascension) and both combined to create 'holy places,' the Islamic case is the exact opposite. Beliefs and piety created religious facts and these, in turn, produced historic facts which, for the contemporary student of religion, culture and even politics, must be
deemed as real as any other kind of 'hard' fact."

'Holy Land of three faiths'. The shrines are either Jewish or Christian; and in any historical consideration a prior claim to their enjoyment would rest with one or the other, or both, of those two religions."[41]

Parkes cited the Patriarchs' Tomb in Hebron – "an ancient Jewish shrine, which was also venerated by Christians," of which "the Muslim sanctuary is largely of crusading or earlier Jewish construction." "We can sometimes trace the actual date and circumstances" in which Muslims seized other shrines from Jews or Christians, "and all alike relate to Jewish or Christian and not to Islamic history." Parkes cited the tombs of Rachel, Samuel, David, Gamliel, Jacob's well, Lazarus' house, the scene of the Ascension, the Cenacle and other sites. "In addition to these shrines, from which in most cases Jews or Christians were wholly or largely excluded after their seizure by the Muslims, Muslims always demanded access to the shrines still left to Jews and Christians."[42]

But the difference in the religions' attachment to the Land runs deeper than shrines. Parkes understood it. Veneration and protection of holy places is the Christian concern. "Christianity has become indigenous in many parts of the world. It is represented by powerful Christian states. There is nowhere a desire of homeless Christians to return to the original land of their religion." Though "for many centuries Islam has been the religion of the majority of its inhabitants and in Jerusalem stands the third holiest shrine for Muslims," still "the homeland of Islam is Arabia," and in a general sense, Palestine is among territories Arabs feel to be the patrimony allotted to them by Allah. Caught between these billion-people religions are the world's maybe fifteen million Jews. Parkes:

"For Jewry has nowhere established another independent national centre; and, as is natural, the Land of Israel is intertwined far more intimately into the religious and historic memories of the people; for their connexion with the country has been of much longer duration – in fact it has been continuous from the second millennium B.C.E. up to modern times – and their religious literature is more intimately connected with its history, its climate and its soil. The Land therefore has provided an emotional centre which has endured through the whole of their period of 'exile', and has led to constant returns or attempted returns, culminating in our own day in the Zionist Movement."[43]

---

[41] Parkes, pp 168-169
[42] Parkes, pp 168-169
[43] Parkes, p 10

5.2.2 Ommayad Dynasty: 660 - 750

Omar died in 644, "carrying to his grave the piety, simplicity, and earnestness which made the reputation, and romance, of the 'Companions' of Mohammed." Islamic unity was soon disrupted. In 656, Othman, the next caliph, was murdered, and Ali, son-in-law of Muhammed, claimed the Caliphate. Mu'awiya, governor of Damascus, accused Ali of the murder, and Ali was assassinated. "With Ali conveniently disposed of, Mu'awiya was acknowledged caliph of all Islam." Thus began the Ommayad dynasty's reign, and the transference of the capital, from Kufa and Medina, to Damascus, with Palestine assuming a "chief state" empire status.[44]

Among Ommayad caliphs (one "ruled briefly, his wife smothering him with a pillow") was Abd el Melek, builder of the Dome of the Rock (adorned with inscriptions "against the Christian doctrines of the Sonship and of the Trinity") and Al Aksa. He failed to raise Jerusalem to rival Mecca,[45] but did make Arabic the official language.[46] His son and successor built Ramleh as Palestine's capital, a status it retained "to the end of the Islamic domination."[47]

DeHaas called the Ommayads "on the whole, of purer Arab blood than their victors," the Abbassids in 750, but they did not repopulate Palestine with ethnically pure desert Arabs:

"The real Arab stock in Islam was exceedingly small, for the people found by the First Companion in Palestine and Syria were a mélange, ethnologically a chaos of all the possible human combinations to which, when Palestine became a land of pilgrimage, a new admixture was added. The myth, that has influenced Near Eastern policies to this day, that there are countless 'sons of the desert,' has no basis in fact. The original tribes which conquered Palestine were small, and, as we have seen, had to draw on forces from various fronts in order to conduct their wars. Moreover, they had to call in the aid of forces that were not Arabic."[48]

Ommayad rule "influenced the Jews considerably." Arabic replaced corrupt Aramaic. Jews simplified Hebrew, adding vowel

---

[44] DeHaas, p 138

[45] DeHaas, pp 139-141

[46] DeHaas, pp 139-144

[47] DeHaas, p. 144. But Bahat noted: "Jewish presence here was continuous until late mediaeval times." Bahat, pp. 26-27. Astonishingly, Ramleh is the *only* Palestine city founded by Arabs. Avi2, p. 161; Vilnay, p. 207.

[48] DeHaas, p. 147. Parkes, p. 65, and Katz, pp. 110-111, likewise call the Ommayads the only purely Arab dynasty.

points. Jewish immigrants who were themselves warrior "sons of the desert" invigorated "the older settled Palestinian Jewish population, which, with its linguistic resources, was an excellent medium for culture exchange." DeHaas quoted Graetz: "'Henceforth the Jews like the Syrian Christians were the channels through which scientific literature reached the Arabs,'" to which he appended "and slowly percolated to the western world."[49]

The majority of the "sons of the desert" themselves, who, storming out of Arabia, had been "part of every great foray that went east, west, north and south," wrote DeHaas, "returned to their desert wastes." "History, song, and story, attest this strange reversion to type, by which the real Arabs disappeared in the sand storms, while a world was conquered in their name, and faith."[50]

5.2.3   Abbasid Dynasty: 750 – 969

"Purely Arab rule, exercised from Damascus by the Omayyad dynasty, lasted a little over a century. The Omayyads were overthrown in 750 by their bitter antagonists, the Abbasids, whose two centuries of government was increasingly dominated first by Persians, then by Turks. When the Abbasids were in turn defeated by the Fatimids, the Arabs had long had no part in the government of the empire, either at the center or in the provinces."[51]

Palestine's "Abbasid" rule was replete with byzantine and once again Byzantine twists. The Abbasids "were placed on the throne by the aid of Persians and Khorassians, and leaned on the swords of the Seljuk Turks." They moved the capital first to Arabia and then Baghdad.[52] "Owing to this transfer of the capital from Damascus, Palestine became somewhat neglected in this period."[53] Peters cited Russian, Turk, Circasian and Kurd influence in

---

[49] DeHaas, p. 149. . See also Katz, pp. 110-111, quoting the eminent Arab historian Hitti: "But when we speak of 'Arab medicine' or 'Arab philosophy' or 'Arab mathematics,' notes Hitti, 'we do not mean the medical science, philosophy or mathematics that are necessarily the product of the Arabian mind or developed by people living in the Arabian peninsula, but that body of knowledge enshrined in books written in the Arabic language by men who flourished chiefly during the caliphate and were themselves Persians, Egyptians or Arabians, Christian, Jewish or Moslem.'"

[50] DeHaas, p 149

[51] Katz, pp 110-111

[52] DeHaas, p. 151

[53] Avi2, p 162

Abbassid rule from Baghdad.[54]   Katz called the Abbasids' two centuries' government increasingly dominated first by Persians, then by Turks.[55]   Parkes wrote of two centuries of disorder that "had its origin at the beginning of the ninth century, when the caliphs began to rely on Turkish mercenaries; for it was not long before these mercenaries and their leaders were in effective control of the state. By the middle of the century the caliphs were little more than prisoners, with a nominally religious primacy, and the governors of provinces were making themselves hereditary and independent princes."[56] Avi-Yonah: "Power was seized by commanders of their Seljuk or Turkish mercenaries, while the caliph became more and more of a puppet."[57]

The western provinces, including Egypt and Palestine, broke away[58] and were ruled by a succession of short-lived non-Arab "dynasties" so bizarre and so unheard of – Tulunides? Ikhshids? – in the West that the first-time reader of an Abbasid history is tempted to believe the author is pulling his leg.

Tulunides

DeHaas: "Abbaside control of Palestine practically ceased after 868, when Ahmed ibn Tulun wrested from his liege lord the independence of Egypt and of Palestine. By that date the Abbasides were little more than the puppets of the Turks; monarchs of the palace-area within their personal vision."[59] Caliph Mutawakkil (847-861), known for having made Christians and Jews wear the "zonarian" garment and suppressing their religious expression was done in by his son in 861, and with this murder, DeHaas wrote, "the great day of the Abbasides passed."[60] In the ensuing unrest,

---

[54]   Peters, p 153

[55]   Katz, pp 110-111

[56]   Parkes, p 76

[57]   Avi2, p 166

[58]   Avi2, p 166

[59]   DeHaas, p 152. Peters: In 878, Ahmad b. Tulun, Turk general and governor of Egypt, conquered Palestine, initiating the reign of Turk Tulunides. See also Avi-Yonah (Av2, p 166): "Ahmed ibn Tulun, the son of a Turkish slave, became the ruler of Egypt and Palestine." And Peters (p 153): In 878, Ahmad b. Tulun, Turk general and governor of Egypt, conquered Palestine, initiating the reign of Turk Tulunides.

[60]   DeHaas, pp 160-161

the Seljuk Turks, "steadily coming to the fore as the controlling influence in the empire," installed a caliph of their choosing.

The Turkish viceroy of Egypt sent there as his deputy one Ahmed ibn Tulun, a former Turkish slave and son of a Turkish slave. By military action and bribery, Tulun became independent ruler of Egypt and Palestine. Tulun rebuilt Acre's harbor and did reconstruction in Jaffa. An inscription on a military road he built still attests to his rule. "This forcible founder of a new dynasty did not disturb his Palestinian subjects, but there exist letters from the Patriarch Theodosius, which indicate that the Christians of the Holy City went in fear of the possible orders of the autocrat."[61]

Following Tulun's death in 884, Tulunides followed each other in rapid succession, ultimately accepting the caliph as suzerain. The last of the Tulunides, and all members of his family, were murdered by the Abbaside caliph, whose general, having gone into Syria to destroy the Carmathians (a marauding pillaging sect named after one Carmat, an involved dwarf "whose deformity provided a name for this new sect"), continued on into Egypt to capture the Tulunides. The general "escorted his captives to Baghdad, where they and he were put to death." "By this means, the Abbasides temporarily recovered possession of Palestine," and "so ended [in the early 900's] a dynasty which combined a series of wars with lavish and ornate ceremonial, and introduced much pomp in its courts during the thirty-seven years of its existence."[62]

Ikhshids

If Tulunide times were bizarre, they were eclipsed by the shortly following interlude of the Ikhshids. Six Abbaside caliphs, "more or less, ruled Palestine, from Damascus or Fustat, according to which governor was stronger, during the thirty years that followed the suppression of the Tulunides, and the rise of the Ikhshids."[63]

The who? From DeHaas, who'd abandoned his Abbasids' chapter and begun one titled "Two Hundred Years of Confusion":

"Disturbances throughout all the provinces of the empire ushered in the tenth century. . . . The Caliph in Baghdad had ceased to influence the affairs of Palestine. In 929, the Carmathians rose again," slaying 30,000

---

[61] DeHaas, pp 160-162
[62] DeHaas, pp 162-164
[63] DeHaas, p 164

Muslims in Mecca and carrying off for a time the Black Stone, sacred symbol of Islam. Around this time, Mohammed ibn Tughf, son of a Turkish slave, freed in childhood, "after an adventurous career" rose through various offices – starting in Egypt as deputy governor, and later rebelling against the governor, and then careening through his own governorships in Amman, Ramleh and Damascus, returning eventually to Egypt. "Here he gave the caliph such obedience that he was made a prince, with a title that the overlords of his homeland had held with great pride – Ikhshid. He thus became the first of a brief, but most impressive and interesting dynasty to rule Palestine."[64]

Two of his sons followed, but in 966 the regent, Abul-Misk Kafur ibn 'Abdallah el-Ikshid, the most capable Ikhshid, became monarch of Syria and Egypt. Karfur, "a negro, native of Abyssinia, with a shiny black skin, great physical prowess, and excellent mental capacity," had been bought as a slave by the first Ikhshid. He went from royal court, to street beggar, to royal court and generalship. The last Ikhshid, one Ahmed, took the throne in 968,[65] only to be overrun by Fatimid invasion of Egypt in 969.[66]

Byzantines

But in that same year, 968, a surprise attack came from a different direction – the Christian west – more than a century before the Crusades. The Byzantines were back. "The Ikhshids were speedily forgotten," DeHaas wrote, when in 968 the Greeks under Phocas and then Zimisces conquered areas of Syria and Palestine, restoring and reopening to pilgrims many churches and shrines.[67] Zimisces wrote the king of Armenia: "At present all Phoenicia, Palestine and Syria are part of our empire, and released from Turkish [sic] servitude."[68] Zimisces' death soon afterwards ended his "ambitious plan to gain more than nominal rule of the lost provinces.... After the departure of the Greeks the inhabitants of Palestine disclaimed their temporary oaths of allegiance, and the Muslims came back to Jerusalem; the Patriarch John VI was burnt alive for presumed support of the Greeks; the Church of the Holy Sepulchre was fired, but no great damage was done."[69]

---

[64] DeHaas, pp 166-167
[65] DeHaas, pp 168-169
[66] DeHaas, p 175
[67] DeHaas, pp 170-171
[68] DeHaas, p 171
[69] DeHaas, p 171

The Abbasid Era Yishuv

What do we know about Palestine's Jews during Prof. Dinur's "Abbasid" Period, 750 to 969?

"The focal point of the Jewish community in the country, the Yeshiva, moved from Tiberias to Jerusalem as a result of an earthquake in 748." Jews working in Temple Mount clothes dyeing lived in the Temple Mount area.[70] In 761 "the small Jewish community in Jerusalem was torn by dissention, supporting or opposing a new Jewish sect, the Ananites (in later generations the Karaites), which had been founded in Persia, and which spread through many of the Jewish settlements."[71] St. Willibald, a pilgrim from Britain, reported that there had been 30 synagogues in Tiberias, which a Michael the Syrian related had been destroyed.

This "St. Willibald" was one of a number of early European Holy Land travelers, some of whose journals are collected in a book published in 1848 by Thomas Wright, *Early Travels In Palestine*. These intrepid travelers' journals testify, though that was not their purpose, making them the more credible for it, to that era's continued Jewish connection to Palestine.

Willibald himself, an Englishman who visited Palestine in the 720's, identified various sites with events in the lives of the Hebrew prophets and observed in the present tense, "Here [in Tiberias] are many churches, and a synagogue of the Jews."[72]

A French bishop named Arculf visited Palestine during early Arab rule in the latter part of the 7th century. His narrative is mentioned by Bede.[73] Arculf associated holy places with Jewish and Christian events and traditions – "the gate of David on the west of Mt. Sion"; "on the spot where the Temple once stood, near the eastern wall, the Saracens have now erected a square house of prayer"; "the place where Abraham raised the altar for the sacrifice of his son Isaac"; the tombs of Rachel and David; and the tombs of the patriarchs in Hebron, within a stream of Christian references.[74]

---

[70] Bahat, pp 26-27
[71] DeHaas, p 155
[72] Wright, p 7
[73] Wright, p xii
[74] Wright, pp 1-7

Bahat in *The Forgotten Generations* included a map of 9th century Palestine Jewish communities and cities with Jewish communities. In the north: Akhziv, Kabrata, Mafshata, Kfar Bar'am, Gush Halav, Elkosh, Sufsaf, Dalton, Kfar Sima'el, Meron, Shazor, Kfar Nahum, Kfar Neborya, Zefat, Yanuh, Beit Dagan, Parod, Akhbari, Akko, Sha'ab, Ma'ariya, Kfar Hannanya, Chorazin, Kabul, Zalmon, Hurok, Mimlah Migdol Nunia, Kfar Hittin, Kfar Tamrata, Kfar Sakhney, Evlayim, Kfar Mandi, Kfar Nimra, Arbel, Mashkana, Rimon, Shefar'am, Tiberias, Beit Me'on, Kfar Manor, Sargonia, Adami, Lubaei, Ardascus, Zippori, Kann'a, Tiv'on, Aithalo, Simoniya, Nazareth, Kfar Agon, Gevat, Yafi'a, Daverat, Ginnegar, Shunem, Tarbenet, Gebal, Kokhav, Beit She'an. In the center and south: Asher, Kfar Saba, Kfar Kasem, Bnei Barak, Ono, Kfar Pegai, Shilo, Tur Shim'on, Lod, Hadid, Gophna, Modi'in, Beit-El, Gimzo, Yafo, Dorin, Kharruba, Beit Horon, Mikhmas, Jericho, Yavne, Emmaus, Ekron, Ashdod, Jerusalem, Beithar, Bethlehem, Ashkelon, Beit Guvrin, Beror Hayil, Gaza, Yutta, Ein Gedi, Eshtomo'a, Carmel, Ma-on. And east of the Jordan: Kamtara, Kurshi, Afek, Zemah, Hamat Goder, Arbel, Geresh, Darela, Adam, Dotha, Medeba.[75]

And 9th century Jews weren't just "there" as unconnected stray individuals, but collectively as the Yishuv. In the 9th century, 800 years after Judaea's destruction, a Gaon declared Palestine's Jews still the valid owners of Palestine's land.[76] A Tiberias rabbi wrote a Hebrew grammar,[77] and Tiberias sages moved their academy, Yeshivat Eretz Israel, back to Jerusalem, "to become the central religious authority for the whole region."[78] The Jerusalem Yeshiva Gaon had "jurisdiction" over all Jews in the Western diaspora, as his Babylon colleague had over the Eastern. Jerusalem's Gaon annually issued the dates of festivals, a ruling in which Babylon sages "yielded superiority to the great Yeshiva in Jerusalem."[79]

"Parallel to this revival of Jewish life and tradition in Jerusalem, another significant event took place: as from the 10th century onward, the Karaite community began arriving in the city, and continued to expand for another

---

[75] Bahat, pp 30-31
[76] JIL, p 203
[77] JIL, p 211
[78] Tal, p 102, quoting Nathan Schur's *History of Jerusalem.*
[79] Tal, p 32. See also Alon, pp 10-12

100

hundred years. In advocating aliyah to Jerusalem they showed even more fervor than others and, in the year 900, their leader, Daniel al-Kumsi, urged each diaspora community to send five representatives to Eretz Israel as forerunners."[80]

10th century Christians joined in attacks on Jerusalem Jews.[81]

Palestine's Ethnic Mix

By the year 900, removed from Arab 638 capture of Jerusalem by 262 years, further than the American Revolution is removed from today, had Palestine become ethnically Arab, even majority Arab?

"... the formation of an integrated Arab majority in the Land was a slow process. Arab historians writing at the end of the ninth and at the beginning of the tenth century (such asYa'quibi and Ibn-Hawqual) indicate that the Arabs did not constitute a majority even in this period, and that the population was still divided into separate ethnic groups."[82]

5.2.4   Fatimid Dynasty: 969 - 1099

"In 969 Palestine again changed its suzerain." Fatimids, claiming lineal descent from Fatima, daughter of Muhammad, early in the 10th century won support in north Africa, invaded Egypt, overwhelming the Ikhshid boy king, and founded a kingdom in a new city, Cairo. In 969, they invaded and took Palestine and Syria.[83]

"Though all the dynastic struggles within the caliphate rested on geneology, all but three of the caliphs were offspring of slave women. With rare exceptions these slave women were of foreign nationality, i.e., alien blood, and obtained by capture, purchase or gift. The Arab strain in the caliphate thus diminished rapidly. To uphold their claims to the throne the Fatimids inverted the Arab theory of descent, for they traced their right to a woman, Fatima."[84]

Palestine Jews "played an important part in the Fatimid conquest." Local Muslims, mostly Sunni, "regarded the Fatimids as blasphemers and usurpers with no right to the caliphate.[85]

"The fortress at Haifa was given to the Jews with the caliph's consent. At the time Haifa was an important Jewish town and seat of the Sanhedrin,

---

[80] Tal, p 33. Katz , p 97: "Tenth century appeals for aliyah by the Karaite leaders in Jerusalem have survived."

[81] JIL, p 205

[82] JIL, p 205

[83] DeHaas, p 175

[84] DeHaas, p. 152. Parkes (p. 76) thought "the claim may have been genuine."

[85] JIL, p 209

and the fact that Jews were allowed to man the fortress there and hold administrative positions confirms that the Yishuv was held in high esteem. Furthermore, it seems that the administration was interested in strengthening the Yishuv and its leadership, and it supported and upheld the authority of the yeshivot and the gaon. The power of the Jewish leaders in this period and their influence on the authorities is emphasized by the fact that local Arab officials and dignitaries repeatedly asked Jews to recommend them to the central administration."[86]

But "though its leaders were honored, on the whole the period was one of decline for the Yishuv." Farming deteriorated toward the 10th century's end.[87] Still, Arab geographer Muqaddasi wrote in 985 of Jerusalem: "Christians numerous ... Everywhere the Christians and the Jews have the upper hand...," that Jews were official money-changers, dyers and tanners.[88] A great many non-Muslims paid the poll tax.[89] Cairo Geniza documents tell of 50 10th-11th century Jewish communities, including all the coastal towns, important inland towns, and small villages; of Jews in Tyre, Galilee, Ramleh, Shefela and the Sharon Valley, Hebron and Gaza; and in Acre, Gush Halav, Dalta and Tiberias.[90] These reveal but "a partial record of the composition and size of the Jewish population of Palestine."[91] Aqaba's Jews had special safeguard for port business.[92]

Jerusalem Jews paid an annual fee,[93] "in return for which the pilgrims were allowed to assemble on the Mount of Olives, and pray facing the Temple ruins."[94] DeHaas surmised that Jewish pilgrims, so welcomed by their brethren, were treated better than Christian. "The city was crowded by Greeks, Copts, Syrians, Georgians, Jacobites, and Armenians — Christians of the East, who regarded

---

[86] JIL, p 209

[87] JIL, p 209

[88] Bahat, pp. 32-34. See also Katz, pp. 90-91. DeHaas (pp. 174-176) writes of Muqaddasi's statement, "Everywhere the Christians and Jews have the upper hand," that "this statement, which surprised the orientalist LeStrange, whose doubts have been copied in many reference works, is fully verified" by evidence of identities of non-Muslim public officials. See also Parkes (p. 96): "...the Arab traveler al Maqdis, who was born in Jerusalem in the second half of the tenth century speaks of the Christians and Jews outnumbering the Muslims in his day."

[89] DeHaas, p 174

[90] Bahat, pp 32-34

[91] JIL, pp 205-206

[92] DeHaas, p 171

[93] DeHaas, p 187

[94] DeHaas, p 180

the visiting Latins as a menace, and who were as capable of attacking the latter, as were the Muslims."[95]

Jerusalem's Rabbanites and Karaites squabbled, causing the caliph in 1024 to intervene. They were ordered to tolerate each other."[96]

The worst Fatimid time for Jews and Christians was under caliph El Hakem, 996-1021.[97] In 1010, the Holy Sepulchre church was destroyed.[98] "Churches were everywhere wrecked and plundered, or converted into mosques. The synagogues in Kjah, Ramleh, and other places, were dealt with in a like manner."[99] And even that situation "deteriorated when the Seljuks took over in 1072 and dominated Jerusalem."[100]

"In 1012, Al-Hakim ordered the forcible conversion of Christians and Jews to Islam, and the resulting persecution in Palestine was fiercer than is generally supposed. The Cordoban scholar and poet Rabbi Yosef Ben Avitur, who was in the country at the time, wrote a dirge on the events that took place. The troops played a major part in the pogroms, and the poet tells of 'pregnant women disemboweled and the blood of old men and babies freely spilt, synagogues destroyed by ravening beasts, victims of the sword in Zion left without burial;' he speaks of rape and ruthless mutilation, of Jews being forced to convert and to 'forget their covenant with their Lord, and their cherished Land.'

"Even though Al-Hakim's decrees were eventually revoked, and the policy of religious toleration restored, the Yishuv was badly hit by the persecution."[101]

But then, crashing upon Palestine's shores like a storm out of the West, bringing death and destruction to Jew and Muslim alike, came the Crusaders.

---

[95] DeHaas, pp 187-188

[96] DeHaas, pp 180-181

[97] JIL p. 210, DeHaas, p. 176, Tal, p. 81

[98] DeHaas, p. 178. See also Tal, p. 81. Parkes (p. 77): "The destruction of a shrine venerated throughout Christendom had serious repercussions in Europe, and prepared the way for the first crusade. Unfortunately it had other repercussions also. The story circulated in the West that it was at the instigation of the Jews that al-Hakim had given the order, and widespread massacres and forced baptisms were the result."

[99] DeHaas, p 178

[100] Tal, p 81

[101] JIL p 210. Jerusalem recovered somewhat. "In 1047, a Persian traveler, Nasir-i-Kursau, wrote in his *Book of Travels*: 'From Byzantium many Christians and Jews come to Jerusalem to visit the churches and synagogues there.'" Tal p 76.

Chapter 6
Christian Crusaders

6.1 Palestine When The Crusaders Arrived
6.2 The Crusader Conquest of Palestine and Palestine's Jews
6.3 The Yishuv During Crusader Times
    6.3.1 Crusader Recognition of Jerusalem's Jewish Connection
    6.3.2 Indigenous Mixed Population Remained
    6.3.3 Defiant Jewish Immigration Continued
    6.3.4 Maimonides
    6.3.5 Travelers' Tales
6.4 Saladin's Defeat of The Crusaders

6.1   Palestine When The Crusaders Arrived

900 years ago, when the "Crusaders" approached the Land they called Holy, having left in their wake a swath of bloodied Jewish communities, news of their coming must have struck deeper fear in the Yishuv[1] than Muslims, with their wide realm to fall back upon. It is no wonder, then, that the Yishuv, incredibly still able to field a cohesive fighting force a millennium after Judaea's destruction, grimly took on the vaunted Crusaders. But let us begin with the Palestine population that greeted them.

---

[1] "The Crusaders' attitude to conquered heretics was presaged by their massacre of Jews in Europe, and their looting of Jewish property, at the start of the Crusades." JIL, p. 212. And see Dinur in JIL, p, 214: "... the Yishuv must surely have heard about the Crusades' beginnings three years earlier, and of the persecution of the Jews in Europe and those encountered en route." Dinur cited evidence from contemporary letters that "the Jews began to have premonitions of the approaching disaster." Bahat (p. 36) wrote that "with the approach of the Crusaders," many Jews left unprotected places in Palestine for Ashkelon, "which was fortified." They appear to have survived. DeHaas (p. 222) recorded that it wasn't until 1153, a half century later, that the Crusaders finally took Ashkelon from the Muslims, and even then under an agreement for "the retirement of the garrison and its wives and children and the Jewish residents, under safe conduct to Egypt." But Bahat (p. 39) wrote that the Jews' remained resident in Ashkelon: "In 1153, Ashkelon, the last stronghold of the Fatimids in Eretz Israel, fell into the hands of the Crusaders, although the Jewish community continued to exist during the Christian occupation of the town. Benjamin of Tudela [c. 1167] found about 200 Rabbinite Jews there as well as 40 Karaites and 300 Samaritans."

"When the Crusaders came to Palestine after 460 years of Arab and non-Arabic Moslem rule, they found an Arabic-speaking population, composed of a dozen races (apart from Jews and Druzes), practicing five versions of Islam and eight of heterodox Christianity."[2]

"At this time, a full thousand years after the fall of the Jewish state, there were Jewish communities all over the country. Fifty of them are known to us [from documents in the Cairo Genizah]; they include Jerusalem, Tiberias, Ramleh, Ashkelon, Caesarea, and Gaza."[3]

6.2   Crusader Conquest of Palestine and Palestine's Jews

"A contemporary Crusader account of the conquest of Jerusalem acknowledges the valor of the Jewish fighters: 'And here, in front of us, were the foreigners, Jew, Turk, and Arab, fighting for their lives with sling-stones, with catapults, with fire and venom . . . and when the end came upon the foreigners, they withdrew from one battlefront, only to find a second battlefront facing them. And though there was terror on all sides, none put down his sword; the Turk, the Arab, and the Jew were among the fallen. The Jew is the last to fall."[4]

"The Jews almost single-handedly defended Haifa against the Crusaders, holding out in the besieged town for a whole month."[5] Albert of Aachen: "Haifa ..which the Jews defended with great courage, to the shame and embarrassment of the Christians."[6] Bahat cites "several chronicles" on "heroism which the Jews of Haifa had been roused to perform." 1719 French priest-historian:

"And Haifa, although moderate in size, was strongly fortified, and, perhaps because of this, for a long time it withstood the mighty onslaught of the Prince Tancred, who attacked it from the sea and also from the land, with the help of the Venetians. Although the Jews fought with courage, they were overcome by the might of the invaders."[7]

"Apart from a few places in the south, we have no information about Jewish participation in the defense of other Palestinian towns; but there is no reason to suppose that Jerusalem and Haifa were exceptional places."[8]

---

[2] Katz, p 112. DeHaas, p 216: "The Latins …had to recognize five types of Muslims (and these were unquestionably of varying descent), as well as the Jews, the Druzes, the Samaritans, and the eight heterodox Christian sects …lines."

[3] Katz, p 90; Bahat, p 37

[4] JIL, p 214

[5] Katz, p 90

[6] Bahat, p 37

[7] Bahat, pp 36-37

[8] JIL, p 215

The Crusaders massacred Jerusalem's Muslims and Jews in an orgy so crimson tales of it chill the blood to this day. DeHaas (p 196): "Seven days of carnage followed the Christian entry into Jerusalem. All eye-witnesses agree as to its horrors and excesses."

"In a letter sent by Godfrey of Bouillon (leader of the first Crusade) to the pope on behalf of 'all the army of God that is in Palestine,' the French Crusader tells of his men riding 'in the corridors and in the Temple of Solomon ... the blood of Saracens as high as the fetlocks of their coursers.' Contemporary records indicate that the carnage was not limited to the actual wars of conquest, or to the battlefield: 'On the third day after the victory, at their commanders' orders, the Crusaders carried out a dreadful massacre of all the people who still survived in the city. The Christians gave themselves wholly to their murderous urges, and not a suckling babe, not an infant, escaped the sword; the streets of Jerusalem were strewn with the corpses of men and women, and the shattered limbs of children.'

"According to the few refugees who managed to escape from the city, 'the Franks killed all the Ishmaelites and Israelites in it.' ... The Jews were given special treatment: 'They were assembled inside their synagogue, which was then put to the fire.'"[9]

"Thus they purified the whole city of its contamination."[10] Hebron and Haifa were "purified" of Jews,[11] and Parkes listed cities where Jews were destroyed.[12] Dinur:

"The Jewish communities in Judaea and those in the towns and villages near Jerusalem suffered the same fate. Fragments of a dirge written in this period (incidentally mentioning Haifa as the city of the Sanhedrin) tell of the destruction of Jaffa, Ono, Lydda, Hebron, Usafiya on Mount Carmel, and Haifa. The last few lines of the manuscript are missing, but presumably they continued the references to other communities that came to the same end."[13]

This is but a sampling of the carnage the Crusaders wreaked when they arrived in their Holy Land. But why had they come? Parkes

---

[9] JIL, p. 214. Others' reports differ in details, but accounts of the atrocity's core are consistent. DeHaas (p. 196 and footnote with sources): "The rabbinical leaders of the Jews had escaped to Damascus, but the congregation was gathered into the synagogue and set on fire; building and human contents were devoured by the flames." Tal (p. 34): "When the Crusaders took Jerusalem in 1099, the members of the Karaite community with their rabbis were driven into a synagogue and were burnt alive, citing Graetz, Vol 6, p. 95, 1894.

[10] JIL, p 214, quoting a Crusader-time bishop.

[11] Bahat, pp 35-36

[12] Parkes, p 97

[13] JIL, p 214

assigned two events as "the direct cause of the first crusade": Seljuk Turks obtaining "complete control of the capital of the Abbasid caliphs" and inflicting a similar defeat on the Fatimids. "The former event compelled a fresh Byzantine appeal to the West; the latter interrupted the pilgrimage from the West to the Holy Land. These two events . . . were the direct cause of the first crusade . . . ."[14] For all the Jews the Crusaders' slaughtered in the Holy Land and en route, it was about Byzantines versus Turks and Turkish interference with Christian pilgrims, not at all about Jews.

6.3   The Yishuv During Crusader Times

6.3.1 Crusader Recognition of Jerusalem's Jewish Connection

A millennium before the Crusaders arrived in Jerusalem, the conquering Romans had destroyed the Jews' Temple, ploughed over their capital, and renamed both capital city and Land, all to obliterate links with the Jews. Half a millennium after the Romans, the conquering Muslims, not by random selection of site, built The Dome of The Rock and Al-Aqsa Mosque on the Jews' Temple Mount. The Crusaders' verdict, rendered 500 years after the Muslims, 1,000 years after the Romans, was that neither attempted obliteration had worked.   The Crusaders "recognized" (Tal's word) the Temple Mount's "historic link to the Hebrew bible," calling the Dome of the Rock the 'Paltium Solomonis' and the vaults beneath it "Solomon's Stables."[15] Though this was of course factually wrong, it was not factually baseless. In 1099, as today, Jewish Temple stonework and living Jewish reverence were present. In 1167, Jewish traveler Benjamin of Tudela recorded:

"Jerusalem has four gates, called the gates of Abraham, David, Sion, and Jehosaphat. The latter stands opposite the place of the holy temple . . . ., In front of it you see the western wall which formed the holy of holies of the ancient temple; it is called the Gate of Mercy, and all Jews resort thither to say their prayers near the wall of the court-yard. At Jerusalem you see also the stables erected by Solomon, and which formed part of his house. Immense stones have been employed in this fabric, the like of which are nowhere else to be met with. You see further to this day the vestiges of the canal near which the sacrifices were slaughtered in ancient times, and all Jews inscribe their name upon an adjacent wall."[16]

---

[14] Parkes, p 82
[15] Tal, p 81
[16] Wright, pp 83-84

6.3.2 Indigenous Mixed Population Remained

After the initial carnage, the Crusaders, like Palestine conquerors before them, settled down to ruling an indigenous tax base, though they barred Muslims and Jews from Jerusalem.[17] Their main revenue source was capitation tax paid by Muslims and Jews.[18] And "all the non-Frank Christians, Syrians, Maronites, Jacobites, Nestorians, Armenians, Georgians, and Iberians, the indigenous Christian population, came under special imposts."[19] But also, there were monopoly grants. "Dyeing, a considerable industry, was generally granted to the Jews."[20]

Tudula: Jerusalem "contains a numerous population, composed of Jacobites, Armenians, Greeks, Georgians, Franks, and indeed people of all tongues," including Jews, "two hundred of whom dwell in one corner of the city, under the Tower of David."[21] DeHaas, quoting Condor: "people of all tongues," including indigo-stained Jewish dyers among people arrayed in garments of all colors.[22]

Dinur: "We know of 10 Jewish settlements in Galilee ... and of Jewish communities in Tiberias and Safad. The largest communities were in the coastal cities of Tyre, Acre and Caesarea."[23]

6.3.3 Defiant Jewish Immigration Continued

Despite the Crusaders' ban on Jewish immigration, Jews continued to come. They came, as Jews have always come, not as pur-

---

[17] Parkes, p 96

[18] DeHass, p 205

[19] DeHaas, p. 204. DeHaas wrote that a "great many records" of the Crusader regime's legal system, 'the famous Assizes of Jerusalem,' based on 'the old code of Justinian,' have survived, expressly referencing the many peoples of the Land. "Saracens, Jews, Greeks (who are termed Grifons or Gryffons), Samaritans, Jacobites, Nestorians, and Herminites, were permitted to appear in a commercial court." "According to Ordinance 221 the Jews were sworn on the Torah." Saracens swore on the Koran, various Christian sects on the cross and holy books, and Samaritans on the "Five Books of Moses." DeHaas, p. 206. During this 12th century Armenians established St James Church in the southwest quadrant of the Old City (see Parkes, p 95), still maintaining their Armenian Quarter today.

[20] DeHaas, p 205

[21] Wright, p. 83. Common misinterpretation of Benjamin's count of Jerusalem's Jews is discussed below.

[22] DeHaas, p 212

[23] JIL, p 215

poseless individuals randomly picking Eretz Yisrael from a map, but as a diaspora magnetically drawn by the homeward pull of the Yishuv. Every Jew who has braved barriers erected expressly to him, from papal edicts banning "transport of Jews to the East" to the WWII and beyond British blockade, stands not as a statistic in a demographer's' book, but as living witness to Eretz as the homeland of Jews. Katz in *Battleground* made the point that though it was the Zionists who began formally counting waves of "aliyah" (immigration) in the 1880's, "only the frame and the capacity for organization were new: The living movement to the land had never ceased," including in Crusader times.

"There were periods when immigration was forbidden absolutely; no Jew could 'legally' or safely enter Palestine while the Crusaders ruled. Yet precisely in that period, Yehuda Halevi, the greatest Hebrew poet of the exile, issued a call to the Jews to emigrate, and many generations drew active inspiration from his teaching. (He himself died soon after his arrival in Jerusalem in 1141, crushed, according to legend, by a Crusader's horse.)"[24]

6.3.4 Maimonides

The giant 12th century scholar Maimonides came to Palestine, but left due to unrest, settling in Egypt, where he became Saladin's court physician and wrote many of his most important works. He died there, but per his request was buried in Tiberias, where his tomb "has been a centre of pilgrimage for Jews ever since."[25]

Maimonides left this testimony, a millennium removed from Judaea's destruction, of the Jews' devotion to their Land: "On the 4th day of Cheshvan we departed from Akko to go up to Jerusalem at grave risk. I entered the great and holy place and prayed there... And just as I was privileged to pray in the Land in its desolation, may I and all Israel live to see its speedy restoration."[26]

6.3.5 Travelers' Tales

Intrepid travelers have left us their experiences in Palestine. Most cited among Jews is Benjamin of Tudela,[27] who visited during Crusader times, in 1167, and recorded counts of the Jews in vil-

---

[24] Katz, p. 97. On the legend of Halevi's death in Jerusalem, see DeHaas, pp. 212-213.
[25] Bahat, p. 39. See also DeHaas, p. 213
[26] Tal, p 76
[27] See, e.g., Parkes, p. 97, Peters, p. 84.

109

lages and towns through which he passed. The fact is that he did not count very many – e.g., 300 each in Shunem and Ashkelon, 200 each in Acre, Caeserea and Jerusalem,[28] 50 each in Alma and Tiberias, fewer in other places. Bahat (p. 40) includes a map with Tudela's counts, to which he appended: "The small numbers undoubtedly reflect the outcome of the destruction of entire communities by the First Crusade, half a century before Benjamin's visit (1167)." Peters (p. 152) cited the Crusades authority Runciman that the Crusaders' massacres had greatly reduced Palestine's Jewish community. But the wonder is not that there were so few Jews in Jerusalem. The wonder is that there were any at all.

Apparently the first Christian pilgrim of whom we have record was an obscure Anglo-Saxon, Saewulf, whose visit Wright placed on the Crusaders' heels in 1102.[29] Saewulf grippingly depicted the dangers of travel from Joppa to Jerusalem "on account of the Saracens,"[30] but what draws our attention to this intrepid 12th century Anglo-Saxon is his linking of Palestine sites with the Jews:

"The entrance to the city of Jerusalem is from the west, under the citadel of King David, by the gate which is called the gate of David"

---

[28] But it appears that one low count – 200 Jews in Jerusalem – typically cited as Benjamin's count, including by Bahat, seems from Benjamin's notes to have been a subset of more. Bahat reproduced a page of Benjamin's manuscript, fortuitously the Jerusalem page, in his book (p. 39), including a translation directly quoting Benjamin as stating that he saw in Jerusalem "a numerous population composed of Jacobites, Armenians, Greeks, Georgians, Franks, and in fact of all tongues. There's a dyeing house rented yearly by the Jews, exclusively. Two hundred OF THOSE JEWS [emphasis added] dwell in one corner of the city, under the Tower of David." In a footnote on page 85 of his *Early Travels in Palestine*, Thomas Wright wrote that in referring to the Jews of Jerusalem, "Benjamin speaks of 200," which, though ambiguous, suggests that Benjamin had counted 200. Fortuitously, like Bahat, Wright, on p. 83, printed a Benjamin translation almost verbatim the same as Bahat's, equally clear on the "200" being a subset of the Jews in Jerusalem: "[Jerusalem] contains a numerous population, composed of Jacobites, Armenians, Greeks, Georgians, Franks, and indeed people of all tongues. The dyeing-house is rented by the year, and the exclusive privilege of dyeing is purchased from the king by the Jews of Jerusalem, TWO HUNDRED OF WHOM [emphasis added] dwell in one corner of the city, under the Tower of David." [Wright, p. 83] See also Tal (p. 102), quoting Benjamin: "TWO HUNDRED OF THOSE JEWS [emphasis added] dwell in one corner of the City, under the Tower of David."
[29] Wright, xix-xxi.
[30] Wright, p 36

"But in the sentences of St. Augustine, we saw that he [Adam] was buried in Hebron, where also the three patriarchs were afterwards buried along with their wives, Abraham with Sarah, Isaac with Rebecca, and Jacob with Leah, as well as the bones of Joseph, which the children of Israel carried with them from Egypt."

"The place where Solomon built the Temple was called anciently Bethel"

"[Near St Anne Church is a] "pool called in Hebrew Bethsaida"

"The river Jordan is four leagues to the east of Jericho. On this side of Jordan is the region called Judea [sic], as far as the Adriatic sea [editor's note says he meant the Mediterranean], that is, to the port of Joppa."[31]

So here is a Crusader era Christian pilgrim piercing the millennium-thick Muslim and Roman veneers back to the Land's Jewish roots – "the citadel of King David," "the gate of David," the Hebron burial sites of the patriarchs and wives and Joseph's bones "which the children of Israel carried with them from Egypt," "the place where Solomon built the Temple," the "pool called in Hebrew Bethsaida," "the city of Jerusalem," and "the region called Judea" between the Jordan and Sea.

6.4   Saladin's Defeat of the Crusaders

The Crusaders were continually defending their kingdom.[32] The decisive lost battle was Horns of Hattin in 1187.[33] Turks led by the Kurd Saladin[34] captured Jerusalem and most of the Land,[35] but the Crusaders didn't give up their kingdom's ghost until 1291.[36]

For all that's always been known of his butchery, an air of gallantry clings in the West to the Crusader's pale ghost. WWII's Supreme Allied Commander titled his memoir *Crusade In Europe*. Today, Muslims take greatest offense to all but condemnatory Western references to the Crusades, but proportionately the Yishuv had been hammered the hardest.[37] But the Yishuv was still present in Palestine when the Crusaders returned home to Europe.

---

[31] Wright, pp 36-45

[32] DeHaas, p 226

[33] DeHaas, p 241

[34] Parkes, p. 80: " . . . the reversion of the country to Islam, when it came, was not to come from Arab sources, but from a fresh wave of Turkish invaders represented by Saladin the Kurd."

[35] Peters, p. 153. See also Tal, p 77

[36] Peters, p 153

[37] Parkes (p. 97): "Proportionally to their numbers, the Jews probably lost more than any other group on the conquest of the country."

111

Chapter 7
Asians, Mongols, Mamluks

7.1　Palestine In The Crusaders' Wake

Migrating to Europe with departing Crusaders offered the Yishuv "no attraction."[1] The post-Crusader period began for the Jews with mixed signals. Their Jerusalem community grew considerably[2] after Saladin issued a proclamation for Jewish refugees from the Crusades to return, spurring immigration and pilgrimage.[3] In 1191, Ashkelon's Jewish community was destroyed by Saladin's Ayyubids. Survivors fled to Jerusalem.[4] Yet in 1211, 300 rabbis moved from England and France to Jerusalem, were received by the king, apparently Saladin's brother, and allowed to build synagogues and colleges, starting an immigration of scholars and pupils from France that continued into the next generation.[5]

In 1229, the Egyptian Sultan gave German Emperor Frederick II Jerusalem for help against his nephew in Damascus. Christians again, but briefly. Soon came Asian and Mongol invaders, followed by Mamluks (aka Mamlukes), who stayed for two centuries.

7.2　The Parade of Asian and Mongol Invaders

"After the Crusaders, there came a period of wild disturbance as first the Kharezmians — an Asian tribe appearing fleetingly on the stage of history

---

[1]　Parkes, p 99. In 1291, the remnants of the Crusader kingdom gave up the ghost. (Peters, p 153)
[2]　Bahat, pp 38-40
[3]　JIL, p. 217. Tal (p. 77) concurred that "Saladin allowed the Jews to return and settle in Jerusalem."
[4]　Bahat, pp 38-40
[5]　Katz, p 97

— and then the Mongol hordes, invaded Palestine. They sowed new ruin and destruction throughout the country. Its cities were laid waste, its lands were burned, its trees were uprooted, the younger part of its population was destroyed."[6]

In 1250, the Mamluks took power in Egypt and Syria,[7] and in 1260 defeated the Mongols at Aix Jelut, adding Palestine.[8]

"Thus arose a type of government for which there is no parallel in history. The Mamlukes were all former slaves of sultans or amirs. At first they were mainly of Turkish origin; after 1390, when the supply of Turkish slaves ran out, they were mostly Circassians from the Caucusus. Each was called by the name of his former owner, and most were converts to Islam."[9]

7.3   The Mamluks

"The Mamlukes were originally mercenaries and slaves in the service of the caliphs of the Egyptian Ayyubid dynasty. In the middle of the 13th Century they overran Egypt and consolidated their rule by defeating the Mongols at Ein Galud (now Ein Harod) in 1263, and by conducting a successful campaign against the remnants of the Crusader armies in Palestine. The campaign ended with Acre's fall in 1291. For 225 years from the fall of Acre to the Ottoman conquest in 1516 — the Mamelukes ruled Palestine, unhampered by outside attacks or by any major internal insurrections . . . "[10]

And so from 1260 to 1516, Palestine was part of the Mamluk Empire, which ruled first from Turkey, then from Egypt.[11] It maintained a mercenary army, mostly Turks and Circassians, controlling the real power through puppet caliphs of Abbasid descent.[12] Of their sultans, Baibars (1260-1277) was the most renowned.[13]

"To the Mamluks, who, in 1250, followed the Crusader Christian interregnum, Palestine had no existence even as a subentity. Its territory was divided administratively, as part of a conquered empire, according to convenience. Its variegated peoples were treated as objects for exploitation, with a mixture of hostility and indifference. Some Arab tribes collaborated with the Mamluks in the numerous internal struggles that marked their rule. But the Arabs had no part or direct influence in the regime. Like all

---

[6] Katz, p 91. See also Tal, p 129, and Parkes, p 102, 153.
[7] Bahat, p 41-43
[8] Peters, p 153
[9] Avi2, pp. 190-191
[10] JIL, p 220
[11] Katz, p 91
[12] JIL, p 220
[13] Parkes, p 102

the other inhabitants of the country, they were conquered subjects and were treated accordingly."[14]

7.4   The Mamluk Era Yishuv

7.4.1   Immigration to New and Revitalized Communities

"Circumstances were by no means conducive to aliya, despite the comparative security; nevertheless [Jewish] immigration to the Land continued throughout the Mamluke period. Sometimes there were many newcomers, sometimes few. But the flow – or trickle – was constant."[15]

There were immigrants from Spain, "on a large scale, to judge from the Spanish royal prohibition of the 'transport of Jews to the East,'" another instance of papal and other European-imposed impediments to specifically Jews' return to their homeland. "For most of the fifteenth century, the Italian maritime states denied Jews the use of ships for getting to Palestine."[16] JIL and Tal: In 1428 the pope blocked Jewish immigrants to the Holy Land.[17] In the 1260's came Rabbi Moshe ben Nahman, "Nahmanides."[18] Finding Jerusalem, destroyed that year by the Tartars, in ruins, he reestablished its Jewish community, started a synagogue, and founded a Yeshiva he later moved to Acre, seat of that period's largest Palestinian Jewish community.[19] Parkes: Nahmanides "managed to revive [Jerusalem's] Jewish community so successfully that there has been no gap in its history from that day to this, and his synagogue for long remained the center of Jewish life."[20]

---

[14] Katz, pp 112-113

[15] JIL, p 222

[16] Katz, pp 98-99

[17] JIL, pp 223-223, Tal p 152. Tales of Jews who did get there were harrowing. In 1479, a pair of amazed Christian pilgrims wrote down that of a Jew newly arrived as an immigrant from Germany, captured by Katz, p. 99. Nor was it easy for Jews who visited Palestine as pilgrims to make their way back. Peters (p 177) cited Christian pilgrims' description of the Jews' difficult, dangerous return route in 1479.

[18] Nahmanides "had defended Judaism with great skill in a religious disputation held before the King of Spain, and published an account of the proceedings – which infuriated church leaders." JIL, pp 217-218.

[19] JIL, p 218

[20] Parkes, p 110. See also Katz, p 91: "Yet the dust of the Mongol hordes, defeated by the Mamluks, had hardly settled when the Jerusalem community, which had been all but exterminated, was reestablished. This was the work of the famous scholar Moses ben Nachman (Nachmanides, the RaMbaN). From the day in 1267 when RaMbaN settled in the city, there was a coherent Jewish community

114

In the second half of that 14th century, many immigrants came from Germany; "many came" after Spanish persecutions in 1391; and in the 15th century many from Italy.[21] Many Jews came to Palestine after the 1492 Spanish expulsion.[22]

7.4.2 Life in the Yishuv's Mamluk Era Communities

Life as not easy for Jews when (and if) they finally reached the land of their fathers. Katz quoted a late 1400's Christian traveler:

" . . . Martin Kabatnik (who did not like Jews), visiting Jerusalem during his pilgrimage, exclaimed: 'The heathens oppress them at their pleasure. They know that the Jews think and say that this is the Holy Land that was promised to them. Those of them who live here are regarded as holy by the other Jews, for in spite of all the tribulations and the agonies they suffer at the hands of the heathen, they refuse to leave the place."[23]

Ashtory Ha-Pari (aka Eshtori Hafarchi), a Jewish geographer in 1322 wrote a Palestine historical-geographical book.[24] 14th century Jewish communities he mentioned include Jerusalem, Gaza, Ramleh, Lod, Beit She'an, Safad, and Gush Halav. Bahat adds: "There is no doubt that there were many more."[25]

Jerusalem

Bahat quoted a Verona monk visiting Palestine in 1335 "that there was a long-established Jewish community at the foot of Mount Zion in the area known as the Jewish Quarter,"[26] and that

"A pilgrim who wished to visit ancient forts and towns in the Holy Land would have been unable to locate these without a good guide who knew the Land well or without one of the Jews who lived there. The Jews were able to recount the history of these places since this knowledge had been handed down from their forefathers and wise men. So when I journeyed overseas I often requested and managed to obtain an excellent guide among the Jews who lived there."[27]

"The Jews who lived there" were uniquely "able to recount the history of these places since this knowledge had been handed

---

in the Old City of Jerusalem until it was driven out, temporarily as it proved, by the British-led Arab Legion from Transjordan nearly seven hundred years later."

[21] JIL, pp. 222-223; Parkes, p. 110.
[22] Parkes, p 110
[23] Katz, p 92
[24] Bahat, p. 44; Tal, p. 103.
[25] Bahat, pp 44-45
[26] Bahat, p 45
[27] Bahat, p. 45.

down from their forefathers and wise men." Ponder that in regard to the Jews' continuing claim to the land as their homeland.[28]

1338 visitor Isaac Ibn Chelo noted "students of medicine, astronomy and mathematics" and "excellent Jewish calligraphers in the city," talents, wrote Tal, evidencing that "secular as well as religious scholarship existed in Jerusalem, even in medieval times."[29]

Both 1384 and 1395 Christian travelers noted that Jerusalem's Jews had their communal residential areas.[30]

A timeline of 15th century Jewish Jerusalem:[31]

1428: Yishuv attempt to buy Mt. Zion buildings blocked by pope

1438: Italian rabbi settled in Jerusalem, becoming spiritual leader

1440: Mamluks imposed tax on Jerusalem's Jews, and many left

1470: 150 Jewish families in Jerusalem

1474: Muslims destroyed an old synagogue, and demanded bribes for a new "Street of the Jews" and "Gate of the Jewish Quarter"

1480: Monk writes of Jews in Jerusalem and Gaza (again in 1484)

1481: Jewish visitor cites Jews in Gaza, Hebron, Jerusalem

1483: Travelers reports of Jews in Jerusalem and Hebron

1488: Rabbi Ovadiah[32] arrives, finds 70 families, many widows

1491: Christian pilgrim: in Jerusalem "not many Christians, but many Jews," who claim the Holy Land, and "refuse to leave." Peters quoted him that there were more Jews than Christians in Jerusalem, and that they consider the country their land.[33]

---

[28] Peters (p 84) likewise regarded this monk's travel guide preference as telling.
[29] Tal, p 208
[30] Bahat, pp 44-45
[31] See Bahat, pp. 47-48; JIL, pp. 222-223
[32] Rabbi Ovadiah from Italy, noted Mishna commentator, founder of a rabbinical college in Jerusalem and head of the 1480's Jerusalem Jewish community: Prof. Dinur said that his writings are a primary source of our knowledge of the Yishuv on the eve of the Spanish expulsion. (JIL, pp 222-223; see also Tal, p. 103; Parkes, p. 111.) And, in a way, centuries later, he contributed yet again to our knowledge of the history of the Yishuv. Tal: "In January 1992, the grave of Rabbi Obadiah of Bertinoro, who had settled in Jerusalem in 1488, was discovered at Silwan — reinforcing a centuries-long Jewish presence in the Old City and its environs." Tal, p 172
[33] Peters, p 176

1495: 200 families, following lifting of Italian ship ban

1496: Destruction and rebuilding of Rambam synagogue

1497: Christian traveler: "In Jerusalem dwell many Jews"

1499: Christian traveler: "...very many Jews in Jerusalem."[34] Katz quoted this pilgrim that the Jews there spoke Hebrew, and another "that they hoped soon to resettle the Holy Land."[35]

A new synagogues ban was in effect; no Jew could erect or repair a house without a special permit (i.e., bribe).

"Time and again Jews were charged with offenses against the Muslim faith and had to buy their way out of trouble. Consequently they were always deep in debt; and if anyone fell behind in his payments his belongings were often auctioned off – even sacred articles and ancient scrolls of the Law. These were usually bought by Christian dealers who sold them in Europe."[36]

Other Cities

Jerusalem was not the Yishuv's main 13th century community. JIL and Bahat identified Acre.[37] Parkes listed Mamluk era Jewish settlement places.[38] Peters cited a "sizeable" Jewish community at Bilbayu.[39] Immigrants from France settled in coastal cities Haifa, Caesarea, Tyre and Acre, but were later forced inland by Mamluk 'scorched earth' destruction aimed at preventing a new Crusader invasion.[40] The Mamluks "totally destroyed" Acre's Jewish community on 1291,[41] and there are records of only a few Mamluk era Jewish families in Caesarea or Hebron. Shechem (Nablus) had "a dozen Jewish families – all that remained from a considerable community that existed before the Arab conquest."[42]

The South

"Throughout the Crusades and the Mamluke period small Jewish communities had managed to hold together in the coastal towns of Gaza, Ash-

---

[34] Tal, p 102.
[35] Katz, p 92
[36] JIL, p 226
[37] Bahat, p 42
[38] Parkes, pp 111-112
[39] Peters, pp 89-90
[40] Bahat, pp 41-42
[41] Bahat, p 42
[42] JIL, p 228

kelon, and Rafa; but by the time of the Turkish invasion only the Gaza community, which had lingered since the era of the Talmud, remained."[43]

Galilee

Yishuv Galilee communities "continued to preserve their traditions." A 13th century Arab geographer noted "groups of Jews from the surrounding region and distant villages" making annual pilgrimage to Shimon bar Yohai's grave in Meron.[44] Bahat took this as evidencing Jewish communities in Galilee despite the Mongol invaders' destruction.[45] Dinur agreed, citing travelers' reports and tax records ("The official lists of Safad's taxpayers for the year 1525-26 name four Jewish quarters"). Rabbi Ovadiah: "The Jews in Safad and Kfar Kana and everywhere else in Galilee are safe and tranquil, and no ill befalls them from the Ishmaelites (Arabs); but the majority are poor, lodging in the villages, peddling their wares in houses, courtyards, and countryside."[46]

7.4.3 Summing Up the Mamluk Era Yishuv

Dinur called the Mamluk period one of Muslim fanaticism, with few Jewish communities – Jerusalem, Mitzpeh, Lydda, Ramleh, Hebron, Gaza, Safad, Beit She'an, and Gush Halav, the largest being Safad (300 families) and Jerusalem (250 families).[47]

"Yet toward the end of the rule of the Mamluks, at the close of the fifteenth century, Christian and Jewish visitors and pilgrims noted the presence of substantial Jewish communities. Even the meager records that survived report nearly thirty Jewish urban and rural communities at the opening of the sixteenth century."[48]

And so the Yishuv survived the Mamluks' misrule, as it had that of the Crusaders, and the waves of Asians and Mongols who had wreaked destruction in the time of turmoil between them. After more than two thousand five hundred years of continuous communally-conscious presence, Palestine's Jews were still there in 1516 to greet, as it were, the next foreign conqueror, the 400-year-staying Ottoman Turks.

---

[43] JIL, pp 227-228

[44] Bahat, p 43. 700 years later, groups of Jews flock to Meron. *Jerusalem Post*, 5/25/05: "Masses Flock to Meron For Lag Ba Omer."

[45] Bahat, p 41

[46] JIL, p 227

[47] JIL, p 222

[48] Katz, p 92

Chapter 8
Turks

8.1 The Fruit of 400 Years of Ottoman Turkish Rule

400 years is a long time in any land's history. 400 years ago, Americans were mostly the Indians. The Palestine that the Ottomans seized from the Mamluks in 1517[29] was mired in misrule. Over 400 years, the Turks made the Mamluks seem enlightened.

The advent of Turkish rule seemed favorable for the Yishuv.

The Ottoman Sultans had encouraged Jewish immigration into their dominions. With their conquest of Palestine, its gates too were opened. Though conditions in Europe made it possible for only a very few Jews to 'get up and go,' a stream of immigrants flowed to Palestine at once. Many who came were refugees from the Inquisition. They comprised a great variety of occupations: they were scholars and artisans and merchants. They filled all the existing Jewish centers. That flow of Jews from abroad injected a new pulse into Jewish life in Palestine in the sixteenth century."[30]

The Yishuv "for a brief while again the center of the whole Jewish world." Sephardim from Spain and Italy soon outnumbered indigenous Arabic-speaking Jews.[31] But it was not to be. Turkish Palestine sank deeper into decay, oppression taking its toll most heavily on the Yishuv.

---

[29] Parkes, p 115
[30] Katz, p 99
[31] Parkes, pp 128-129

"The Ottomans, to whom Palestine was merely a source of revenue, began to exploit the Jews' fierce attachment to Palestine. They were consequently made to pay a heavy price for living there. They were taxed beyond measure and were subjected to a system of arbitrary fines."[32]

If Palestine's Arabs expected favorable treatment, as against the Land's Christians and Jews, under its rule by their fellow Muslims, they were soon disabused of such hopes: "Their [Palestinian Arabs'] state did not improve under the Ottoman Turks. The fact of a common Moslem religion did not confer on the Arabs any privileges, let alone any share in government. The Ottomans even replaced Arabic with Turkish as the language of the country."[33]

As Turk misrule wore on, the cumulative centuries of corruption, neglect, oppression, ruinous taxation, lawlessness, murderous hatred and other abuses sunk the country to its lowest population not just of Turkish but of all historical times. Parkes had Palestine's inhabitants looking back to the Mamluks almost with nostalgia:

"The insecurity created by the complete indifference of the Turkish pashas to the local wars and raids of local amirs, bedouin tribes, Druzes and others, was reducing not only the Jewish community, but the whole country to a degree of poverty and desolation even greater than it had known under the Mamluks. Traveler after traveler reports desert and marsh where there had been fertile fields, and ruins where there had been towns and villages. But even so, the country had not yet sunk to its lowest level. It was in the early part of the nineteenth century that the cumulative effect of centuries of neglect and destruction reached its culmination."[34]

Katz cited some of these "traveler after traveler" reports. Reports on Palestine in the late 18th and throughout the 19th century are filled with its emptiness, its desolation: Thomas Shaw in 1738; Constantine Volney in 1785; Alexander Keith, c. 1840, who, recalling Volney's description of a "ruined" and "desolate" country, added that the land in Volney's day "had not fully reached its last degree of desolation and depopulation." 1835, Lamartine:

"Outside the gates of Jerusalem we saw indeed no living object, heard no living sound, we found the same void, the same silence . . . as we should have expected before the entombed gates of Pompeii or Herculaneum . . . a complete eternal silence reigns in the town, on the highways, in the country . . . the tomb of a whole people."

---

[32] Katz, pp 94-95
[33] Katz, p 113
[34] Parkes, pp 131-132

And bleakest of all, Mark Twain in *The Innocents Abroad* in 1867:

"Desolate country whose soil is rich enough, but is given over wholly to weeds – a silent mournful expanse. . . . A desolation is here that not even imagination can grace with the pomp of life and action. We reached Tabor safely. . . . We never saw a human being on the whole route. . . .

"There was hardly a tree or a shrub anywhere. Even the olive and the cactus, those fast friends of a worthless soil, had almost deserted the country. . . .

"Palestine sits in sackcloth and ashes. Over it broods the spell of a curse that has withered its fields and fettered its energies. Palestine is desolate and unlovely. . . .Palestine is no more of this workday world. It is sacred to poetry and tradition, it is dreamland."[35]

Tolkien did not paint a more mournful portrait of Mordor.

What was Palestine's population nadir and when did it sink to it?

"By Volney's estimates in 1785, there were no more than 200,000 people in the country. In the middle of the nineteenth century, the estimated population for the whole of Palestine was between 50,000 and 100,000 people."[36]

"Palestine was gradually emptied of people between 1512 and 1800. The low point was probably reached in 1850, when estimates varied between fifty and one hundred thousand."[37]

8.2   The Rise of Nationalism Among Arabs and Jews

But then, with accelerating momentum, the Yishuv began to revive and move into the sunlight of modern times. The late 19th century Zionist movement invigorated the Yishuv, but the Zionists encountered a revival already at work. The Yishuv had stirred before, but now in a way it had not done since Bar Kochba, to take back the Land. True, homeland Jews had fought alongside the Persians 500 years after Bar Kochba, and soon again with the Arabs, and a half a millennium later against the Crusaders, but in each of those wars, the Yishuv – for all the desperate courage it mustered – had fielded a homegrown militia in a world-class clash of empires. Awakened and reinvigorated by Zionists, it grasped the possibility of fulfillment of the dream of generations for Israel's redemption. It grasped, too, that such redemption would come, this side of the Messiah, only if Jews brought it themselves.

---

[35]   All quoted in Katz, pp 108-109

[36]   Katz, pp 108-109, citing sources.

[37]   DeHaas, p 39n

121

Simultaneous Arab nationalism was different, being mostly pan-Arab at first. Late Jerusalem Post Editor David Bar-Illan:

"The Arab residents of this country during the British mandate [i.e., even after the Ottoman era] resented the appellation Palestinian. They called themselves Arab, and named all their institutions – from the Arab Higher Committee on down —'Arab,' not Palestinian. Only the Jews, when referring to themselves and their institutions in English,[38] used the name Palestinian: The Palestine Post (still the incorporated name of this newspaper), the Palestine Symphony, the United Palestine Appeal are typical examples. . . . "

Applying the term Palestinian to Arabs of Palestine probably began in the early 1960's, but neither Security Council resolution 242 of 1967 nor 338 of 1973 mentions Palestinians at all. It was only in the mid-seventies that the term became popular."[39]

But despite Arab historian Hitti's insistence that "there is no such thing as Palestine history,"[40] there were some Arabs in Palestine who felt there was. Conor Cruise O'Brien in *The Siege* (pp. 119-120) cited a 1914 appeal by an Arab challenging "the Zionists desire to settle in this country and expel us from it." This Arab argued that though Jews had "dwelt in this holy land in former times, God sent them from it" and they "deserted it for two thousand years." – precisely the attack of which Parkes warned. O'Brien also quoted the concluding words of Christian Arab nationalist George Antonious' 1938 "famous" book, *The Arab Awakening*: "No room can be made in Palestine for a second nation except by dislodging or exterminating the nation in possession." But O'Brien assessed that the development of the two Palestinian nationalisms had not been "symmetrical," that "a Palestinian nation was not something which the Zionists found awaiting them; it was something that came into being, first slowly and then frantically, in response to Zionism itself."[41]

The Zionists were arriving back, not to an Arab Palestine state, which had never existed in history, but to an 18-centuries' foreign-ruled land which had just sunk to its lowest population in historic times. It was not a land which Jews had ever "deserted," let alone

---

[38] Diaspora summer camp kids of the 1948 era, this author included, enthusiastically sang dining hall verses, all ending in "Fight, Fight, Fight for Palestine!"
[39] See David Bar-Illan "Eye on the Media" column, Jerusalem Post, May 24, 1991; compiled in Bar-Illan, "Eye on the Media," pp. 166-67.
[40] See Bar-Illan, pp 166-167
[41] O'Brien, p 120

"for two thousand years." Beyond that they had "dwelt in this holy land in former times," they had dwelt there in Jewish sovereignty twice. It had been the Jews' conception of holiness that had imparted holiness to the land, a holiness recognized by the Arab conqueror who had built a mosque on the Jews' Temple Mount a millennium and a half after the Jews had built there the first of their Temples. During those long dark Hadrian-to-Herzl centuries no native state, Arab or other, came into being there. The next native state after Jewish Judaea's fall in 135 was Jewish Israel in 1948.

8.3 The Yishuv During Ottoman Times

The perception that the only Jews in Palestine during Ottoman times were a few aged, other-worldly pious paupers dependent on diaspora alms is flat wrong. In even their holy cities like Safad, as in agricultural areas like Galilee villages, the Jews – merchants, farmers, artisans, smiths – were industrious indigenous people of the land who confronted "every discouragement" with worldly along with religiously-grounded resources. The main centers of Ottoman era Jewish life were the four holy cities of Jerusalem, Safad, Tiberias and Hebron. The largest of these, and the Yishuv's spiritual center during much of this era, was Safad.[42]

8.3.1 Safad

"At the height of their splendor, in the first generations after their conquest of Palestine in 1516, the Ottoman Turks were tolerant and showed a friendly face to the Jews. During the sixteenth century, there developed a new effervescence in the life of the Jews in the country. Thirty communities, urban and rural, are recorded at the opening of the Ottoman era. They include Haifa, Sh'chem, Hebron, Ramleh, Jaffa, Gaza, Jerusalem, and many in the north. Their center was Safed . . . ."[43]

Safad's Jewish merchants were gold and silversmiths, weavers, knitters, dyers and merchants.[44] Its 10,000 Jews, Palestine's largest Jewish community, traded in spices, cheese, oil, vegetables and fruit.[45] Safad, large, worldly and economically secure, "assumed the recognized spiritual leadership of the whole Jewish world":

---

[42] Bahat, 50-52
[43] Katz, p 93
[44] JIL, p 232
[45] BAHAT, p. 50. Parkes (p. 129) cited Safad Jewish population of c. 15,000 at one point in the sixteenth century. Peters (p. 178) cited the British Peel Commission that Safad "contained as many as 15,000 Jews in the sixteenth century."

The luster of the 'golden age' that now developed shone over the whole country and has inspired Jewish spiritual life to the present day. It was there and then that a phenomenal group of mystic philosophers evolved the mysteries of the Cabala. It was at that time and in the inspiration of the place that Joseph Caro compiled the Shulhan Aruch, the formidable codification of Jewish observance, which largely guides orthodox custom to this day. Poets and writers flourished. Safed achieved a fusion of scholarship and piety with trade, commerce, and agriculture. In the town, Jews developed a number of branches of trade. Lying halfway between Damascus and Sidon on the Mediterranean coast, Safed gained special importance in the commercial relations in the area. The 8,000 or 10,000 Jews in Safed in 1555 grew to 20,000 or 30,000 by the end of the century."[46]

Safad had a yeshiva in 1524,[47] and in 1577 Palestine's first Hebrew printing press.[48] Its 16th century synagogues have been in use to the present.[49] "The official lists of Safad's taxpayers for the year 1525-26 name four Jewish quarters," one of "old" inhabitants of continuous residence.[50] In 1549, the Turks built and garrisoned a surrounding wall, and the Jews built a huge fortified khan with houses for 100 families, shops, and warehouses. "For nearly 100 years this remained their place of refuge in times of violence."[51]

This hopeful Turkish rule start there didn't last. A chilling incident was Sultan Murad III's (1575-1595) order to deport 1000 wealthy Safad Jewish families to Cypus.[52] In 1567, Bedouin and Druze burst into and ransacked the town. In 1576 (the deportation order year), the Yishuv protested local Safad officials' extortion and cruelty. The Sublime Porte ordered an inquiry, "but the defiant local governors continued to do as they pleased."[53] "In the early 17th century Christian visitors described life in Safed for the Jews: 'Life here is the poorest and most miserable that one can imagine.'

---

[46] Katz (p. 93), citng historian H.H. Ben-Sasson in Hebrew. See also Peters (p. 178) that "at the turn of the century, the Jewish population had grown from 8,000-10,000 (in 1555) to between 20,000 and 30,000 souls."

[47] JIL, p 233

[48] Katz, p 94

[49] See Bahat, pp 50-55, including photos

[50] JIL, p 227

[51] JIL, pp 228-233

[52] Ben Zvi wrote that he later rescinded the order. JIL, p. 236. But Katz (p. 94), citing Lewis, wrote that the deportation order was issued twice, in 1576 and 1577, and that "it is not known whether they were in fact deported or reprieved."

[53] JIL, p 237

Because of the harshness of Turkish rule and its crippling *dhimmi* oppressions, the Jews 'pay for the very air they breathe.'"[54]

In 1587, Safad was plundered again and the printing press destroyed. In 1599, it was hit by drought, plague and famine. An appeal was made to the Diaspora, to which European and Istanbul Jewish communities responded, but in 1602 the plague came again, and in 1604 once more the Druze. In 1628, the Druze seized the town again, for several years "oppressing and despoiling the small Jewish population." In 1636, the Damascus pasha ousted the Druze, "but the victors were as bad as the vanquished had been." That same year the Druze came back, devastating the town again, and in a conflict amongst them "both factions plundered the Jews of Safad." Most fled.[55] The Cabala masters had already gone to other Yishuv Holy Cities, Hebron and Jerusalem.[56]

17th and 18th century travelers listed Safad among Jewish communities.[57] In 1777, 300 immigrants gave "added impetus" to Jewish settlement, and Safad's synagogues grew from 11 to 30.[58] But Parkes wrote that it was impossible to restore the ground that had been lost.[59] In 1799 Safad was sacked by the Turks.[60] Still, during an 1810-1816 stay, historian Burkhardt recorded:

"The town is built upon several low hills, which divide it into different quarters; of these the largest is inhabited exclusively by Jews, who esteem Szaffad as a sacred place. The whole may contain six hundred houses, of which one hundred and fifty belong to the Jews, and from eighty to one hundred to the Christians."[61]

Jews were attacked in Safad and elsewhere in 1834 and in 1837 Safad suffered an earthquake.[62] Still, in 1839, British consul

---

[54] Peters (p. 178), referring to John Hayman and Joseph Egmont, in "Travels" published in London in 1759, also quoted by Katz, p. 93, citing Ish-Shalom.

[55] JIL, pp 237-238

[56] JIL, p 241

[57] Katz, p 95

[58] Bahat, p 58

[59] Parkes, pp 131-132

[60] Peters, p 179

[61] Peters, p 181. However, in 1815, around this same time, an English diplomat and writer named Turner wrote what he was told by Catholic monks: "[Safad] contains, they said, from 1,000 to the 1,500 homes, of which from 300 to 350 are Jewish and the rest Turkish." (Bahat, pp. 60-61)

[62] Peters. p 182-183

Young stated Safad's Jewish population at 1500.[63] Peters reported Jewish majorities in Safad and Tiberias by 1851.[64]

8.3.2   Galilee

For long periods, Safad has had a Galilee hinterland.[65] Katz:

"In the neighboring [to Safad] Galilean countryside, a number of Jewish villages — from Turkish sources we know of ten of them — continued to occupy themselves with the production of wheat and barley and cotton, vegetables and olives, vines and fruit, pulse and sesame." [citing Bernard Lewis, 'Notes and Documents From the Turkish Authorities,' p. 15 ff]

"The recurrent references in the sketchy records that have survived suggest that in some of those Galilean villages — such as Kfar Alma, Ein Zeitim, Biria, Pekiin, Kfar Hanania, Kfar Kana, Kfar Yassif — the Jews, against all logic and in defiance of the pressures and exactions and confiscations of generation after generation of foreign conquerors, had succeeded in clinging to the land for fifteen centuries." [citing Yitzhak Ben-Zvi in Hebrew]. Now, for several decades of benevolent Ottoman rule, the Jewish communities flourished in village and town."[66]

"By 1549 there were at least a dozen Jewish settlements in Galilee, three urban, the rest rural."   Ben Zvi, in *The Jews in Their Land,* showed our knowledge today of those villages, including of Pekiin, "the only one of these ancient Jewish settlements where Jewish families have continued to live up to our own time."[67]

Pierre Belon, a French doctor who traveled in Galilee in 1547:

"We look around Lake Tiberias and see the villages of Beth Saida and Korazim. Today Jews are living in these villages and they have built up again all the places around the lake, started fishing industries and have once again made the earth fruitful, where once it was desolate."[68]

Katz wrote that 17th and 18th century Jews still tilled the soil in Galilean villages,"[69] but Ben Zvi painted a gloomier picture:

---

[63] Bahat, p 63

[64] Peters, p 199

[65] "Jewish agriculture took on new life as Safad flourished. The rabbis turned their attention to the agricultural laws, and proclaimed a fallow year in 5264 (1503-04) according to the reckoning of Maimonides, the reckoning still followed today." JIL, p. 235.

[66] Katz, pp 93-94

[67] JIL, pp 232-235

[68] Bahat, p 52

[69] Katz, p 95

"Gradually, hunger, disease and pillage exhausted Galilee and almost erased the 16th century Jewish villages. Only faint traces of Peki'in and Kfar Yassif were left. The Jewish farmers of Kfar Alma, Kfar Hanania, Kfar Kana, Kfar Kabul, and Julas (Julis) were gone. Historians of the time mentioned Jewish merchants and peddlers still living in the countryside of Upper Galilee, but their allusions were generally to the fate of some un-happy traveler, murdered by fellahin or Bedouin."[70]

In the 17th century, many Jews left Galilee for Jerusalem, which was experiencing a Jewish revival,[71] but Galilee settlement was renewed in the first half of the 18th, as in Kfar Yassif, a religious agricultural village whose residents left in 1707 and returned in 1747.[72] According to British Consul Young's 1839 population count and two private ones, the Jewish population at that time of Safad, Tiberias and the Galilee villages was a very few thousand.[73] Yet this must be seen in context of the land's diminished popula-tion, a quarter million, including Turks, Greeks, Maronite and Catholic Christians, along with Muslim Arabs and Jews.[74]

8.3.3   Tiberias

"In 1549, a Christian tourist found a tiny impoverished Jewish community in Tiberias. But there were soon great changes, thanks to Donna Grazia Mendez and her son-in-law Don Joseph Nasi, wealthy Marranos who'd escaped the Inquisition and settled in Turkey, where Don Joseph had distinguished himself at the Sul-tan's court. They worked on restoring Tiberias as a Jewish center. Sultan Sulieman, builder of Jerusalem's walls standing today, ap-proved their plan, and their envoy arrived in Tiberias in 1563.[75]

The envoy began a wall for the town's defense, but once again Yishuv self-defense plans were thwarted by others. First the pope, encouraged by Palestine Christians, conspired with the grand vi-zier to thwart the restoration. Then a local sheik frightened off Arab workers by declaring the wall would mean the end of Islam. Nonetheless, with the Damascus pasha's aid, the almost mile-long wall around the town was completed in 1564. Next, Jews repaired

---

[70] JIL, p 238
[71] Bahat, pp 53-54
[72] Bahat, pp 56-58
[73] Bahat, pp 59-63
[74] Bahat, p 63
[75] JIL, p 237

old houses and built new ones, "and soon Tiberias had blossomed into a prosperous Jewish town and an important center of learning."[76] In 1600 an English priest who visited with a group of English pilgrims, recorded in *The Travels of Four Englishmen and a Preacher*: "Tiberias, the town that Salim gave to Graziola, a Jewish grande dame, is entirely occupied by Jews."[77]

Here, too, the 16th century's revival and prosperity did not last. "In 1660, the town was destroyed completely, and for the next 80 years Jewish Tiberias lay in ruins,"[78] having been "sacked," like Safad, "by bedouins and Druzes in succession." Bahat: "There are accounts that Tiberias was abandoned in 1670 because of the ruthlessness of the Turks."[79] But with its resettlement by Jews 80 years later, "Tiberias became again one of the four Holy Cities."[80]

British Consul Young counted 600-700 Tiberias Jews, and a Scottish theologian 1200, in 1839,[81] but as early as 1817 an English traveler wrote: "It is said that the number of people living in Tiberias is 4,000, of which two-thirds are Jews."[82] Peters stated that Jews were again the majority in Tiberias, as in Safad, by 1851.[83]

8.3.4 Jerusalem

Muslim Persecution and the Staying-Power of the Yishuv

"In the early years of the Ottoman occupation, the Jews of Jerusalem endured a great deal of slander and official troublemaking and had to pay heavy bribes" for survival. Documents tell of extortion and trade restrictions, such as Jewish merchants being forbidden to sell in the square, causing many Jerusalem Jews to move to Safad.

---

[76] JIL, p. 237. See also Parkes, p. 130, and Bahat, pp. 50-52.

[77] Bahat, p 52

[78] JIL, p 238

[79] Bahat, p 54

[80] Parkes, p 131. Peters tells that the return to Tiberias came when the ruling sheik invited a Smyrna rabbi "to 'come and inherit the land of his ancestors.' The rabbi's grandfather had been 'Rabbi of Tiberias' a century earlier and his arrival in 1742 brought back the Jewish community of Tiberias, which had been virtually purged of Jews for seventy years." Peters, p 179. See also Bahat, pp 56-58.

[81] Gilbert, p 12

[82] Bahat, p 61

[83] Peters, p 199

Things improved under Sulieman (1520-1566).[84] Between 1536 and 1542 he built the walls and pools of Solomon, repaired sewers and cisterns. Jews returned,[85] living in quarters coterminous with the Jewish Quarter of our time.[86] Ulrich Prefat of Slovenia's chronicle for 1546-47: "Many Jews dwell in Jerusalem and there is a special street of the Jews."[87]

Bahat, showing synagogue photographs, described a religious-site link between Jerusalem's 16th century Jews and today's:

"When the Jews were expelled from Spain in 1492 many found their way to the Turkish empire, where they succeeded in attaining high positions. Their influence helped many Spanish Jews to settle in Jerusalem after 1516. The newcomers built a new synagogue, named Eliyahu Hanavi, and soon afterwards three more synagogues were built. This group of four synagogues still exists (though used as a garbage dump during the Jordanian occupation of 1948-67), and is once again restored."[88]

These Sephardim were only one of Jerusalem's Jewish groups.

"… there were four congregations: Sephardi, Ashkenazi, Moroccan (North African), and Musta'arabim. The largest was the Sephardi, with its exiles from Spain and Portugal. Next came the Ashkenazi, comprised of 15 very old families (descendants of Jews who had come in the days of Maimonides) as well as more recent arrivals from Europe, including immigrants from Italy. The Musta'arabim . . . were descendants of the Land's early inhabitants."[09]

Jerusalem's was a vibrant Jewish community. "In 1587 a rabbi wrote: ' The Land is steeped in learning as it never was in ancient days. There is a religious school (Talmud Torah) with more than a hundred youngsters ... also a college'…"[90]

But towards the 16th century's end, Abu Sufain became governor of Jerusalem and things worsened. In 1586, the 3-century-old

---

[84] Parkes, p 116
[85] The official census of 1526 showed 200 Jewish householders. By 1539 one source has 224 householders and 19 bachelors, and by 1555, 324 householders and 13 bachelors. JIL, pp 230-231. Apparently, a "household" was a 4-to-5 person family, for Bahat states: "According to official censuses in the second quarter of the [sixteenth] century, the number of Jews in Jerusalem varied between approximately 1,000 and 1,500. Bahat, p 51
[86] Bahat, p 51
[87] Tal, p 102
[88] Bahat, p 51
[89] JIL, p 228
[90] JIL, p 238

129

Nahmanides synagogue was taken and turned into an Arab warehouse.[91] Oppression and onerous taxation worsened from there.[92] "There was a typical incident in 1643: the governor inflicted a burdensome tax on the community, and since the community was quite incapable of paying it, he jailed all its notables. . . . This happened again and again during the period, forcing the Jews to leave the city. By 1663 most of them had gone to Ramleh, abandoning their property in Jerusalem." The oppression wasn't even all rational. In 1637, Muslims threatened to kill Jerusalem's Jews unless rain came in three days (it did).[93]

"The Jews of Jerusalem, wrote the Jesuit Father Michael Naud in 1674, were agreed about one thing: 'paying heavily to the Turk for their right to stay here.... They prefer being prisoners in Jerusalem to enjoying the freedom they could acquire elsewhere.... The love of the Jews for the Holy Land, which they lost through their betrayal (of Christ), is unbelievable. Many of them come from Europe to find a little comfort, though the yoke is heavy.'"[94]

"The custom of extorting money from pilgrims remained unchanged for centuries, as told in 1751 by a Swedish traveler, Frederick Hasselquist: 'As 4,000 persons (Christians) besides as many Jews come from all quarters of the world, this sum (a total of 25 piasters for each pilgrim) may be esteemed a considerable revenue for the Turks; and indeed they receive no other from this uncultivated and almost uninhabited country.'"[95]

Tal quoted Francois Rene de Chateaubriand in *Journal of Jerusalem*, 1811: "Christians and Jews alike lived in great poverty and in conditions of great deprivation. There are not many Christians but there are many Jews and these the Muslims persecute in many ways."[96] Peters quoted an 1834 letter that a 40,000 strong Muslim mob "'rushed on Jerusalem . . . The mob entered, and looted the city for five or six days. The Jews were the worst sufferers, their

---

[91] JIL, p 231
[92] See Peters, p. 178, documenting that Jerusalem Jews were "bitterly persecuted" and on at least one occasion "a great number of them were massacred" by local Turkish rulers in the seventeenth century.
[93] JIL, p 240
[94] Katz, p. 95, citing Ish-Shalom.
[95] Tal, p 82
[96] Tal, p 155

homes were sacked and their women violated."'[97] Turn to virtually any page of Peters' chapter "*Dhimmi* in the Holy Land" for a
litany of like persecutions of Jews and Christians during the Ottoman era. At one point, after detailing numerous brutal incidents:

"In the following few decades (1848-1878) scores of incidents involving
anti-Jewish violence, persecution and extortions filled page after page of
documented reports from the British Consulate in Jerusalem. A chronology would be overwhelming, but perhaps a few extracts [see Peters, p.
191 ff] from those complaints will show the pattern of terror that continued
right into the period of the major Jewish immigration beginning about
1878."[98]

Tal quoted an 1843 traveler: "In Jerusalem, his (the Jew's) case is
a very hard one. He is oppressed and robbed by the Turks in a
most unmerciful manner; in short, for him there is neither law nor
justice."[99] And Karl Marx in 1854: "Nothing equals the misery and
suffering of the Jews who are the constant object of Muslim oppression and intolerance."[100]

A restraining factor in Muslim-on-*Dhimmi* Jerusalem violence was
this, quoted by Peters from an 1859 British consulate document:

"'The Mohammedans of Jerusalem are less fanatical than in many other
places, owing to the circumstances of their numbers scarcely exceeding
one quarter of the whole population –and of their being surpassed in
wealth (except among the Effendi class) in trade and manufactures by
both Jews and Christians.'"[101]

Jewish determination not to be driven from Jerusalem prevailed.
Bahat quoted a 1656 monk: "In Jerusalem there also live many
Jews who came from all over the world."[102] Ben Zvi referred to
the anonymous author of a famous letter, "Hurvot Yerushalayim"
("The Ruins of Jerusalem"): "More of our people now inhabit the
city of our Lord than have done so since Israel was exiled from its
Land. Daily many Jews come to settle there, in addition to the pilgrims who come to pray to Him who stands beyond our Wall
…'"[103] In 1700, Rabbi Judah the Pious led 1,000 Jews from Po-

---

[97] Peters, p 183
[98] Peters, p 191
[99] Tal, p 155, citing Gilbert's Jerusalem History Atlas.
[100] Tal, p 155
[101] Peters, p 198
[102] Bahat, pp 53-54
[103] JIL, p 239

131

land who settled in Jerusalem and began building the Hurva synagogue. In 1751, the Kabbalist Shalom Sharabi came from Yemen. "In 1777, Rabbi Isaiah Bardaki arrived from Poland to become leader of the Jewish community and Austrian vice-consul."[104]

Mark Twain, *The Innocents Abroad* (1869), caught the intensity of the Jews' attachment to Jerusalem: "'Everywhere precious remains of Solomon's Temple. That portion of the ancient wall ... which is called the Jews' Place of Wailing, where the Hebrews assemble every Friday to kiss the venerated stones and weep over the fallen greatness of Zion.'"[105]

Jerusalem's Jewish Majority Throughout Modern Times

Jerusalem's Jewish majority didn't begin in 1967, 1948 or during the Mandate, but in Ottoman times. We'll look at some figures and then combine them into tables showing that Jews had become Jerusalem's largest population segment before the Zionists came.

Parkes wrote that around 1830

"the Jews probably numbered about 3,000 out of a total population of 11,000. Ten years after [first British Consul Young's 1939] arrival a Christian deputation from Malta's Protestant College gives a total population of 15,000 with Muslims at 6,000, Jews at 5,000, and Christians at 4,000. In 1872 the Jewish population just outnumbered the combined Christian and Muslim inhabitants (Jews 10,600, Christians, 5,300, Muslims 5,000). In 1899, the comparable figures were: Jews 30,000, Christians 10,900, and Muslims 7,700."[106]

Gilbert's 1838 figures show a total Jerusalem population of less than 16,000, with Jews already the largest segment – 6,000 Jews, 5,000 Muslims and 3,000 Christians. His 1896 figures – 28,000 Jews, 8,700 Christians, 8,600 Muslims, of a total Jerusalem population of 45,300[107] – agree with Parkes' in showing more Jerusalem Jews than Christians and Muslims combined.

Peters cited an 1856 letter by British Consul Finn that Jerusalem's Jews "greatly exceed the Moslems in number."[108]

---

[104] Tal, p 103

[105] Quoted in Tal, p 78

[106] Parkes, p 230

[107] Gilbert, pp. xi-xii, 1. He cited (p. 12) Consul Young's 1839 count of Jerusalem Jews as more than 5,500.

[108] Peters, p 199

Look again at that remarkable 1859 British Consulate document quoted above:

"'The Mohammedans of Jerusalem are less fanatical than in many other places, owing to the circumstances of their numbers scarcely exceeding **one quarter of the whole population** –and of their being surpassed in wealth (except among the Effendi class) in trade and manufactures by both Jews and Christians.'"[109] (emphasis added)

1864 British records: "The population of the city of Jerusalem is computed at 18,000 of whom about 5000 are Moslems, 8000 to 9000 Jews, and the rest Christians of various denominations."[110]

Bahat cited the 1839 counts of Jerusalem's Jews by Consul Young and the Scottish clergyman, respectively, at 5,000 – 6,000, and 6,000 – 7,000.[111] He cited an 1855 English missionary as stating Jerusalem's then Jewish population at 11,000, confirmed, said Bahat, by British Consul James Finn in 1878 in *Stirring Times.*[112]

Tal's *Whose Jerusalem?* lists its Jews, Muslims and Christians at various modern times. 1820-21: "For the first time Jews made up the largest ethnic group as recorded by noted travelers." 1838: 6,000 Jews, 5,000 Muslims, 3,000 Christians. 1844: 7,120 Jews, 5,760 Muslims, 3,390 Christians. 1876: 12,000 Jews, 7,560 Muslims, 5,470 Christians. 1909: 45,000 Jews, 12,000 Muslims, 10,200 Christians. 1911: 30,800 Jews, 10,000 Muslims, 15,000 Christians. 1948: 99,320 Jews, 36,680 Muslims, 31,300 Christians. 1990: 353,200 Jews, 124,200 Muslims, 14,000 Christians.[113]

Tal quoted Karl Marx in the International Herald Tribune, April 15, 1854: "The sedentary population of Jerusalem number about 15,000 souls, of whom 4,000 are Muslim and 8,000 are Jews."[114] He quoted the July 15, 1899, Pittsburgh Dispatch: "Thirty thousand out of 40,000 people in Jerusalem are Jews...."[115]

---

[109] Peters, p 198
[110] Peters, footnote 37 on p. 501, quoting British report.
[111] Bahat, p 63
[112] Bahat, pp 64-65
[113] Tal, p 94
[114] Tal, p 155
[115] Tal; p 103

Jerusalem's Population in the 19th and 20th Centuries

Source	Year	Jews	Muslims	Christians	Total
Parkes	1830	3,000			11,000
Gilbert	1838	6,000	5,000	3,000	14,000
Tal	1838	6,000	5,000	3,000	14,000
British Consul Young (Bahat)	1839	5,500			
Scottish Clergyman (Bahat)	1839	6,500			
Malta College (Parkes)	1840	5,000	6,000	4,000	15,000
Tal	1844	7,120	5,760	3,390	16,270
Karl Marx (Tal)	1854	8,000	4,000	3,000	15,000
Clergyman Bartlett (Bahat)	1855	11,000			
British (Peters)	1864	8,500	5,000	4,500	18,000
Parkes	1872	10,600	5,000	5,300	20,900
Tal	1876	12,000	7,560	5,470	25,030
British Consul Finn (Bahat)	1878	11,000			
Gilbert	1896	28,000	8,600	8,700	45,300
Parkes	1899	30,000	7,700	10,900	48.600
Tal	1911	30,800	10,000	15,000	55,800
Tal (pre-state)	1948	99,320	36,680	31,300	167,300
Tal	1990	353,200	124,200	14,000	491,400

Pct of Jerusalem's Population in the 19th and 20th Centuries

Source	Year	Jews	Muslims	Christians	Total
Parkes	1830	27			100
Gilbert	1838	43	36	21	100
Tal	1838	43	36	21	100
British Consul Young (Bahat)	1839				
Scottish Clergyman (Bahat)	1839				
Malta College (Parkes)	1840	33	40	27	100
Tal	1844	44	35	21	100
Karl Marx (Tal)	1854	53	27	20	100
Clergyman Bartlett (Bahat)	1855				
British (Peters)	1864	47	28	25	100
Parkes	1872	51	24	25	100
Tal	1876	48	30	22	100
British Consul Finn (Bahat)	1878				
Gilbert	1896	62	19	19	100
Parkes	1899	62	16	22	100
Tal	1911	55	18	27	100
Tal (pre-state)	1948	59	22	19	100
Tal	1990	72	25	3	100

Conclusions we can draw from these tables from multiple sources are [1] that Jerusalem's Jews were a plurality over Muslims and Christians before the mid-19th century, perhaps by the 1830's, a half century preceding the Zionist movement and more than a century before Israel's statehood; and [2] that by the 19th century's end the Jews had become and remained the city's majority.

The Beginnings of Modern Jerusalem

But who were these 19th century Jerusalem Jews? A famed British archeologist's 19th century economic survey dispels any myths that 19th century Jerusalem Jews were but ghostly mourners of an ancient destruction. For all their reverent remembrance of Jerusalem's Jewish past, they lived a vibrant and practical life in their own time, at their city's economic and demographic hub. Tal:

"With the 19th century, a new era dawned for Jerusalem's economy. Charles Warren, the famous British archeologist (who carried out excavations in the city in 1867/68) conducted the first survey on the city's trades and here are some of his findings: apart from 108 Jewish shopkeepers (of a total of 332), many Jewish artisans followed a number of diverse trades — 83 shoemakers (out of 230), 11 carpenters (out of 36), 15 silversmiths (out of 57) and 10 bakers (out of 77). There were also 77 professional letter-writers in the city, all of them Jewish, yet there were no Jews among the 86 coffin makers. Jews of oriental origin, particularly those from Kurdistan, showed a preference for physically more demanding occupations, such as porters and stone-cutters. These facts clearly contradict the myth that 19th century Jerusalem Jews were either old men praying at the Western Wall or religious youth studying the Torah."[116]

In 1857, Laemle's Girls' School opened in Jerusalem; in 1865, the Evelina de Rothschild School for Girls; in 1882, the Alliance Israelite Universelle.[117]

But it was a different 19th century action, also initiated by Jews, that burst the demographic constraints of Jerusalem's 16th century walls, creating, unequivocally, modern Jerusalem:

"The congested Old City covered a mere 245 acres . . . . The Jews were the first to take the lead by moving out of the city walls. Comprising the majority of inhabitants, they were the first to suffer from living in crowded quarters and under intolerable sanitary conditions . . . ."[118]

In 1855, Moses Montefiore acquired a plot outside the city's western wall. The community Mishkenot Shananim was built on it, using funds Judah Touro provided. Montefiore also built there a windmill, never used for its intended purpose, but one of Jerusalem's best-known landmarks today. Oriental Jews' building of the small Mahane Israel community followed, and then two large-scale developments, Nahlat Shiva (named after its seven founders,

---

[116] Tal, pp 232-233
[117] Tal, p 208
[118] Tal, pp 162-164

135

members of some of the city's oldest established families), and the ultra-orthodox Me'a She'arim, by far the largest quarter, comprising 300 dwelling units.[119] Yemin Moshe, adjacent to Mishknot Shananim, was built in 1894, named after Montefiore.[120]

There was more to all this than merely moving from the "old" city to the "new." Jerusalem's three hundred year old walls were functional, not ornamental, in a lawless time and place of particular insecurity for non-Muslims, and initial settlement in the new Jerusalem communities outside the walls "was accomplished only by the endeavor of the more courageous among the city's Jews."[121]

8.3.5   Hebron

Hebron, site of the Cave of Machpelah with its tombs of the Patriarchs, is the fourth of the Yishuv's four Holy Cities. Ben Zvi:

"The small Hebron [Jewish] community had survived since Mamluke days; and in fact the Jewish quarter, a courtyard surrounded by stone houses, was not abandoned until the massacres of 1929. In the sixteenth century, Hebron was an important place of pilgrimage and, small though its Jewish community was, it included a number of renowned rabbis and biblical scholars who had come from Safad and Jerusalem to be near the tombs of the Patriarchs."[122]

A distinguished 1486 pilgrim, Dean of the Mainz Cathedral, wrote Jerusalem's and Hebron's Jews "will treat you in full fidelity – more so than anyone else in those countries of the unbelievers."[123]

The Yishuv in Hebron, bolstered by Inquisition refugees, exhibited the Yishuv's characteristic resilience. Peters: "The Holy Land's throbbing, spirited Jewish life continued, even in Hebron, where [quoting Gilbert] 'the prosperous Jewish community . . . had been plundered, many Jews killed and the survivors forced to flee' in 1518, three years after Ottoman rule began. By 1540, Hebron's Jewry had recovered and reconstructed its Jewish Quarter...."[124]

Both tenacious Jewish presence and persistent Muslim persecution of the Jews of Hebron continued through the Ottoman era.

---

[119] Tal, pp 162-163
[120] Bahat, p 60
[121] Bahat, p 60
[122] JIL, p 232
[123] Peters, p 85
[124] Peters, p 85

First, continued Jewish presence: A 1631 Christian writer listed Hebron along with Jerusalem, Gaza, Haifa, Ramleh, Nablus, Safad, Acre and Sidon making up some 15,000 Jews in the country.[125] Ben Zvi wrote that by 1662 condition of Jewish life had become so bad that Hebron, along with Jerusalem, Gaza and Ramleh, had become the places where "almost the whole of Palestine Jewry was concentrated."[126] 17th century Hebron included Ashkenazim and Kabbalists. Its Holy City status attracted immigrants.[127] Travelers reported the small Karaite community had ceased to exist, but other Jewish sects took over its synagogues and properties.[128] Travelers reported Jews in Hebron in the 17th-18th centuries,[129] and British Consul Young in the 19th,[130] where they remained until driven out by Muslims in the bloody pogrom of 1929.

Second, continued Muslim harassment: In Hebron, "in addition to the regular exactions, threats of deportation, arrests, violence, and bloodshed, the Jews suffered the gruesome tribulations of a blood libel in 1775."[131] Peters, citing multiple sources, referred to Hebron Jews being massacred in 1834 by soldiers from Egypt sent to put down a local Muslim rebellion.[132] Peters cited British records of vicious Muslim persecution of Jews in Hebron and elsewhere in the 1840's and 1850's, including through oppressive and brutal governmental involvement.[133]

Parkes' verdict was that the Hebron community, struggling "with isolation and with the constant repression of local rulers and Bedouin tribes, though never wiped out . . . never succeeded in becoming prosperous."[134] But "prosperous" or not, the Yishuv resided in its holy city Hebron when the Ottomans came in the 16th century, and when the Ottomans left in the 20th.

---

[125] Bahat, pp 53-54
[126] JIL, p 242
[127] Peters, p 199
[128] JIL, p 243
[129] Katz, p 95
[130] Gilbert, p 12
[131] Katz, p 95
[132] Peters, p 183
[133] Peters, pp 191-193
[134] Parkes, p 131, a judgment perhaps inconsistent in part with Gilbert's, as cited by Peters, above, that the Yishuv had been "prosperous" in Hebron in pre-Ottoman days.

8.3.6 Elsewhere in The Land

Gaza

Gaza is among the Yishuv communities cited by Ben Zvi at the start of the Ottoman era.[135] It was strengthened by refugees from Spain. "The Jews of Gaza were mostly merchants who flourished at this crossroads of the great caravan route to Egypt. Others cultivated vineyards and manufactured wine."[136] Through the Crusader and Mamluk periods, Gaza had been among small southern Jewish coastal communities, including Ashkelon and Rafah, but by the Turkish invasion only Gaza, dating from the Talmudic era, remained.[137] Parkes called it the Jews' "only flourishing community" in the south.[138] 17th-18th century travelers cited Jews there.[139] Ben Zvi listed Gaza among the few cities where the Yishuv was "concentrated" during dark 17th century times.[140]

Shechem (Nablus)

Ben Zvi listed Shechem among Yishuv communities extant at the Turkish invasion. But "unlike Gaza, the ancient town of Shechem was impoverished," with a quite small Jewish community.[141] Still, it hung on. 17th-18th century travelers mentioned it.[142]

Ramleh

Ramleh, to which 1600's Jerusalem Jews fled when unable to pay oppressive taxes repeatedly imposed on their community,[143] was a city 17th-18th century travelers noted as having resident Jews.[144]

Other Ottoman Era Yishuv Communities

17th-18th century travelers and Western diplomats also noted Jews in Acre, Sidon, Tyre, Haifa, Jaffa, Irsuf, Caesarea and El Arish.[145] And there were Jews in the land whom travelers did not see. Ba-

---

[135] JIL, p 232
[136] JIL, p 232
[137] JIL, p 227
[138] Parkes, p 131
[139] Katz, p. 95. See also Bahat, pp. 53-54.
[140] JIL, p 242
[141] JIL, p 232
[142] Katz, p. 95; Bahat, pp. 53-54
[143] JIL, pp 240-242
[144] Katz, p. 95; Bahat, pp. 53-54
[145] Katz,p. 95; Bahat, p. 54

hat cited 17th century Turkish tax maps, which "tell us of the existence of Jewish farmers in the most remote parts of Palestine."[146]

The Jews were not scattered, inconsequential individuals living in the Palestine society's shadows with no influence on life in the land, but prominent in the foreground and integrally involved in the Palestine society's life. A Spanish Fransican monk in 1665: "There are large numbers of Jews everywhere." A Dutch scholar's 1667 compilation of travelers' descriptions of their journeys: "There are Jews all over Syria and the Holy Land, especially in Acre, Sidon, Damascus, Jerusalem, Hebron and Gaza. No transactions take place without the knowledge of the Jews and even the smallest dealings pass through their hands."[147]

8.4 The 19th Century Revival of the Yishuv

At the 18th century's end, Napolean, invading Palestine, issued his famous appeal to Palestine's Jews to rise up and reclaim the land of their fathers. The Yishuv didn't bite. But who knows whether Napolean's stirring appeal didn't continue to resonate in the heads of Palestine's Jews long after he himself had gone from the land? In any case, driven by awakening forces in the Jewish world both within and outside the land, fundamental change occurred in the Yishuv in the 19th century. Katz captured a sense of it, in referring to immigrants of 1810, disciples of the Vilna Gaon, as "one of the last links in the long chain bridging the gap between the exile of their people and its independence. They or their children lived to see the beginnings of the modern restoration of the country."[148]

It was not until 1897 that Theodor Herzl convened the First Zionist Congress in Basle, Switzerland. The Zionist movement had already begun with pioneers from Russia dedicating themselves to reclaiming The Land by reclaiming the land,[149] but even before them the Yishuv was stirring inside the land. The mid-19th century Yishuv-led breakout from Jerusalem's 16th century walls, was followed, inter alia, by the 1870 establishment of Palestine's first

---

[146] Bahat, p 54
[147] Bahat, p 55
[148] Katz, p. 101
[149] Tal, p 233

modern agricultural school at Mikveh Israel, near Jaffa,[150] and in the same year the establishment of the village of Motza, near Jerusalem,[151] and in 1878, the founding by Jerusalem Jews of The Land's first modern Jewish agricultural settlement, Petah Tikva, each exemplifying the pre-Zionist revival of the Yishuv.

Vilnay captured the spirit of the Petah Tikva volunteers in his incomparable Guide:

"Petah Tikva – Door of Hope, the oldest Jewish agricultural settlement in Israel, is often referred to as 'Em Hamoshavot' – Mother of the agricultural settlements. It was founded in 1878 by Jews from Jerusalem who believed that tending the soil would redeem Israel. The name Petah Tikva was chosen in accordance with the prophesy of Hosea: 'and I will give her vineyards from thence, and the Valley of Achor for a door of hope (petah tikva), and she shall respond there, as in the days of her youth.' The Achor Valley is located in the vicinity of Jericho in the Jordan plain. The settlers' first intention was to build their colony within its boundaries; and although they could not purchase land in this region, eventually settling in the Jaffa area, they retained the name Petah Tikva, which epitomized their aspirations. From their very first days, hardships and ordeals were the lot of the pioneers, who found in these remote surroundings vast malarial swamps. Although many fell victim, the survivors continued with their constructive efforts until they saw their labor bear fruit, when Petah Tikva, the marshes drained, blossomed into a great center of citrusculture – a basic element in its development."[152]

It was to this already reviving Yishuv that, beginning in the 1880's, the Zionists came. Certainly, they brought an influx of vitality and a mindset of modern practicality to the Yishuv, but their "aliyah" ("going up to The Land") was hardly unprecedented. They followed in the footsteps of countless generations of Jews Returning before them:

"Modern Zionism did indeed start the count of the waves of immigration after 1882, but only the frame and the capacity for organization were new: The living movement to the land had never ceased."[153]

Travel of Jews to Palestine has always been fraught with difficulties and dangers confronting all audacious travelers in every era, but superimposed upon them, from decrees of medieval popes to the British blockade, have been obstacles placed uniquely for

---

[150] Katz, p 101
[151] Bahat, p 64, Vilnay, p 188
[152] Vilnay, pp 243-244
[153] Katz, p 97

Jews. Inside the land – ruled for two millennia from afar by Romans, Byzantines, Arabs fading to Turks, Crusaders, Mamluks, Ottoman Turks, and finally British – it is Palestine's Jews, the Yishuv, that has faced "every discouragement." And still they are there. Just, as Bahat noted, that it was "the more courageous among the city's Jews" who led the breakout from Jerusalem's medieval walls, so too it has been "the bolder spirits" among persecuted diaspora Jews, buffeted from place to place, who in every age have made their way Home. E.g.,

"In the middle of the seventeenth century, there passed through the Jewish people an electric current of self-identification and intensified affinity with its homeland. For the first time in Eastern Europe, which had given shelter to their ancestors fleeing from persecution in the West, rebelling Cossacks in 1648 and 1649 subjected the Jews to massacre as fierce as any in Jewish history. Impoverished and helpless, the survivors fled to the nearest refuge – now once more in Western Europe. Again the bolder spirits among them made their way to Palestine."[154]

And so too has it been in every age the presence, beacon, magnet of the Yishuv, at times diminished to a pummeled minor minority, that has made the millennia-long return of countless generations of Jews possible, even thinkable, and formed the continuous generational link between ancient Israelites and Israelis today.

---

[154] Katz, pp 99-100

Chapter 9
Israel Again

How the Yishuv, fortified by Zionist and other immigrants, developed politically, economically and militarily into an Israel able to throw back and then some the Arab invasion to strangle it on the day of its proclamation of re-established Jewish sovereignty in Israel, ending a political but not presence hiatus of eighteen hundred years, is a chapter of Yishuv history worthy in courage against invaders of all the chapters that came before. There are numerous honorable accounts of it, by Israelis and others.

This book has traced how the Jewish people arrived or arose in Canaan in the late second millennium BCE; how Israel and Judah careened through the Iron Age and finally fell to mighty Assyrian and Babylonian empires; how those who had remained and returned to Yehud rebuilt the Temple, threw off Alexander's Seleucid successors and re-established Jewish independence under the Maccabees-Hasmoneans, only to crash headlong into Rome; how the Yishuv survived and even flourished religiously during its ensuing Talmudic Age; how it joined militarily in Persian and Muslim Empires' clashes with the Romans' Byzantine heirs, and lived during the Muslim dynastic era; how the Yishuv militarily took on the invading Crusaders and survived the Crusader era; how it survived Mongols and Mamluks and 400 years of Ottoman Turkish oppression; and how toward the end of that benighted Ottoman era, the Yishuv burst into the sunlight of modern times.

In 1897, with the Yishuv already breaking out of Jerusalem's medieval walls, founding new communities, and pioneer immigrants of the "first" aliyah already at work reclaiming the Land by reclaiming the land, Theodor Herzl convened the First Zionist Congress in Basel, Switzerland. Afterwards, he confided to his diary:

"If I were to sum up the Congress in a word – which I shall take care not to publish – it would be this: At Basel I founded the Jewish State.

"If I said this aloud today, I would be greeted by universal laughter. In five years, perhaps, and certainly in fifty years, everyone will perceive it."[1]

---

[1] Herzl's diary entry for September 3, 1897; quoted in JIL, p 279

And in 1947, fifty years to the year, through Palestine's partition by the UN into Arab and Jewish states, everyone did.

And then, finally, in the lengthening shadows of erev Shabbat, Friday, May 14, 1948, an aging leader rose and faced an assembled crowd and, standing beneath Herzl's portrait, began reading an extraordinary document. It proclaimed the independence of a people in a place neither of which had seen such status since this very people had defended and lost its independence there eighteen hundred years earlier. "His face shone as the passages rolled sonorously from his lips, and took on life and form."[2]

"The Land of Israel was the birthplace of the Jewish people . . . Here their spiritual, religious and national identity was formed. Here they achieved independence and created a culture of national and universal significance . . . wrote and gave the Bible to the world. . . ."

The aging leader, Zionist to the core, read on that "exiled from the Land of Israel, the Jewish people remained faithful to it in all the countries of their dispersion, never ceasing to pray and hope for their return and the restoration of their national freedom"; that "impelled by this historic association, Jews strove throughout the centuries to go back to the land of their fathers and regain their statehood"; that "in recent decades, they returned in their masses. They reclaimed the wilderness, revived their language, built cities and villages." The document cited the First Zionist Congress' proclamation, the League of Nations Mandate granting "explicit international recognition of the historic connection of the Jewish people with Palestine and their right to reconstitute their National Home"; the UN Partition Resolution, and "the natural right of the Jewish people, like any other people, to control their own destiny in their sovereign State."

All these foundations of Israel cited that day in that historic document were, as Sharef called the UN Resolution, "unassailable." Yet, the aging leader might have appended one more: The Jewish people's "real title deeds" had been written, in Blood & Fire, by the "heroic endurance of those who had maintained a Jewish presence in The Land all through the centuries, and in spite of every discouragement."

---

[2] Zeev Sharef, *Three Days,* p. 282. See also Ben-Gurion, *Israel: A Personal History,* p. 80-81

Index

Index

Index

Index

Index

Index

Index

Index

Index

Index

Sion, 99, 107 (see also
  Zion)
Sitz im Leben, 15
Six Day War, 4, 35, 74
Sochoh (see Socho)
Socoh, Sochoh, 29, 41
Solomon, King, 1, 13-15, 17, 21, 23-27,
  31, 33, 42, 67, 85, 90-91, 106-107,
  111, 129, 132
Solomon, Pools of, 129
Solomon's Stables, 107
Sophronious, Patriarch, 88, 90
Spain, Spanish, 114-115, 119, 129,
  138-139
Spanish Expulsion, 115
St. Anne's Church, 111
Stager, Archeologist, 15
Strabo, 58
Strato's Tower, 60 (see also Caesarea)
Sufain, Abu, 129
Sunni, 101
Switzerland, 139, 142
Synagogues, 63, 68-72, 75-76, 80,
  82-83, 88, 99, 103, 106, 112, 114,
  116-117, 124-125, 129-130, 132, 137
Syria, 15, 24, 44, 51-52, 57, 59-60,
  63-64, 66, 76, 89, 94, 97-98, 101, 113,
  139
Syrian, 56, 86, 95, 99, 102, 108
Tabor, 64, 121
Tal, Eliyahu, 31, 34, 86, 91, 106, 109,
  114, 116, 131, 133, 135
Talmud, 68-69, 72, 77, 80, 82, 118
Tancred, Prince, 105
Tanner, 102
Tarbenet, 100
Tartars, 114
Tel Aviv University, 25
Tel Zayit, 16-17, 27
Temple Mount, 31, 33, 58-59, 64, 86,
  88-91, 99, 107, 123
Temple, Second, 20, 47, 49-50, 57-58,
  62-63, 75

Temples, Jewish, 1, 14-15, 18, 20, 22,
  31, 33, 37-39, 42, 44-64, 66, 69, 72,
  75, 79-80, 84-86, 88-92, 99, 102,
  106-107, 111, 123, 132, 142
Tenth Legion, 66
Theodosius, 82, 97
Thubron, Colin, 90-91
Tiberias, 62-63, 69-70, 82, 87-88,
  99-100, 102, 105, 108-110, 119, 123,
  126-128
Tirat Tsevi, 71
Titus, 64, 84
Tiv'on, 100
Torah, 52-54, 58, 63, 79-80, 135
Touro, Judah, 135
Transjordan (see Jordan)
Travelers, 99, 104, 107, 109, 115-118,
  120, 125, 127-128, 130-131, 133,
  137-140
Trojan War, 14
Tsipori, 68 (see also Sepphoris)
Tughf, Mohammed ibn, 98
Tulunide Dynasty, 96-97
Tunnel, 39-40
Tur Shim'on, 100
Turkey, 113, 127
Turkish, 73, 96-98, 107, 113, 118-120,
  124-126, 129, 138-139, 142
Turks, 84, 86, 95-97, 105, 107, 111,
  113, 118-120, 123-125, 127-128,
  130-131, 141
Twain, Mark, 121, 132
Tyre, 102, 108, 117, 138
UN (see United Nations)
United Nations, 143 (see also UN)
United Palestine Appeal, 74, 122
Unleavened Bread, Feast of, 19 (see
  also Passover, Pesach)
Ur, 52
Urusalem, City of, 23 (see also
  Jerusalem)
Usafiya, 106
Ussishkin, David, 25

Index

Authorities Cited

ALON, Gedalish Alon, *The Jews In Their Land In the Talmudic Age*, Cambridge, Harvard University Press (1984)

AVI, Michael Avi-Yonah (ed.), *A History of the Holy Land*, Jerusalem, Jerusalem Publishing House Ltd (1969)

AVI2, Michael Avi-Yonah, *The Holy Land: Architecture, Sculpture, Painting*, New York, Holt, Rinehart and Winston (1972)

BAHAT, Dan Bahat, *The Forgotten Generations*, Jerusalem, The Israel Economist (1975)

BAR-ILLAN, David Bar-Illan, *Eye On The Media*, Jerusalem, Jerusalem Post (1993)

BEN-GURION (cited herein as "JIL"), David Ben-Gurion (ed.), *The Jews In Their Land*, Conceived and Edited By David Ben-Gurion, Garden City, Doubleday & Company (1966)

DEVAUX, Roland de Vaux, *Ancient Israel: Its Life and Institutions*, Grand Rapids, William B. Errdmans Publishing Company (1977) (orig. French ed. 1958)

DEHAAS, Jacob de Haas, *History of Palestine: The Last Two Thousand Years*, New York, MacMillan Company (1934)

DEVER, William G. Dever, *Who Were The Early Israelites And Where Did They Come From?*, Grand Rapids, William B. Errdmans Publishing Company (2003)

DEVER2, William G. Dever, *What Did TheBible Writers Know and When Did They Know It?: What Archeology Can Tell Us about the Reality ofAncient Israel*, Grand Rapids, William B. Errdmans Publishing Company (2001)

FINKELSTEIN, Israel Finkelstein and Neil Asher Silberman, *The Bible Unearthed: Archeology's New Vision of Ancient Israel and The Origin Of Its Sacred Texts*, New York, Simon & Schuster (2001)

FRIEDMAN, Richard Elliott Friedman, *The Bible With Sources Revealed*, New York, Harper Collins Publishers (2003)

GILBERT, Martin Gilbert, *Jerusalem: Rebirth of a City*, New York, Viking Penguin (1985)

GRAETZ, Heinrich Graetz, *History of The Jews,* Philadelphia, Jewish Publication Society (1956) (orig. ed. 1891)

HERZOG, Chaim Herzog and Mordechai Gichon, *Battles of the Bible*, London, Greenhill Books (rev. ed. 2002)

HOFFMEIER, James K. Hoffmeier, *Israel In Egypt: The Evidence for the Authenticity of the Exodus Tradition*, New York, Oxford University Press (1996)

ISSERLIN, B.S.J. Isserlin, *The Israelites*, London, Thames & Hudson (1998)

KATZ, Samuel Katz, *Battleground: Fact & Fantasy In Palestine,* New York, Steimatzky-Shapolsky, (Updated Steimatsky ed., 1985)

KONNER, Melvin Konner, *Unsettled: An Anthropology of The Jews,* New York, Viking Compass (2003)

LOWENTHAL, Marvin Lowenthal (trans.), *The Diaries of Theodor Herzl,* New York, Dial Press (1956)

NETANYAHU, Benjamin Netanyahu, *A Durable Peace: Israel and Its Place Among The Nations,* New York, Warner Books (2000)

NEUSNER, Jacob Neusner, *First Century Judaism In Crisis,* New York, Abingdon Press (1975)

O'BRIEN, Connor Cruise O'Brien, *The Siege: The Saga of Israel and Zionism,* New York, Simon & Schuster (1986)

PARKES, James Parkes, *Whose Land? A History of the Peoples Of Palestine,* New York, Taplinger Publishing Company (1971)

PETERS, Joan Peters, *From Time Immemorial: The Origins of the Arab-Jewish Conflict Over Palestine,* New York, Harper & Row (1984)

PRITCHARD, James B. Pritchard, *Gibeon: Where The Sun Stood Still, The Discovery of the Biblical City,* Princeton, Princeton University Press (1962)

SCHAUSS, Hayyim Schauss, *The Jewish Festivals, From Their Beginnings To Our Own Day,* New York, Union of American Hebrew Congregations (9th printing, 1961)

SHAREF, Zeev Sharef, *Three Days*, New York, Doubleday & Company (1962)

TAL, Eliyahu Tal, *Whose Jerusalem*, Jerusalem, International Forum For A United Jerusalem (1994)

THUBRON, Colin Thubron, *Jerusalem*, London, George Rainbird Ltd (1977)

VILNAY, Zev Vilnay, *The Guide To Israel*, Jerusalem, Zev Vilnay (16th ed., 1973)

WHITLEY, Charles Francis Whitley, *The Exilic Age*, Philadelphia, The Westminster Press (1957)

WILKEN, Robert L. Wilken, *The Land Called Holy: Palestine In Christian History & Thought*, New Haven, Yale University Press (1992)

WRIGHT, Thomas Wright, *Early Travels In Palestine*, New York, Ktav Publishing House (1968) (first published in 1848)

YADIN, Yigael Yadin, *The Message of The Scrolls*, New York, Grosset & Dunlap (1962)

A SAMPLE OF OTHER POPULAR BOOKS FROM PAVILION PRESS:

The authors and editors of Pavilion Press are generally available for speaking engagements. For specific information, contact us at webmaster@pavilionpress.com and refer to the web site for further information. www.pavilionpress.com.

MURDER THRILLER - *LETHAL RHYTHM* by Dr. Peter Kowey and Marion Fox.
Philip Sarkis was a good doctor—maybe a little too good. So when he is sued for malpractice after a young patient dies suddenly and unexpectedly, he sinks into an alcoholic depression, losing his family and his career. With the help of two remarkable women attorneys, Sarkis discovers some astonishing things about his patient, her husband and his diabolical mistress, and himself.

MIDDLE EAST - *ISRAEL 3000* - *by Jerome Verlin.*
Just how long have Jews continuously lived in Israel? Even since the battle of Jericho, and that is a long time, over 3000 years. In meticulous detail and using historical and archeological discoveries, the book documents the this habitation and asks the question, shouldn't Israel celebrate it's 3200 anniversary?

Jane Austen - a whole series.
From books that can not be found anywhere else, like *Jane Austen's Letters, Great Illustrations*, and Her *Homes and Friends* to her wonderful novels, this is the place for Austen lovers.

ADVENTURE BIOGRAPHY - *SURVIVOR FROM AN UNKNOWN WAR* by Stephen Crane
You only really know about WWII, The Soviet Union, romance, and breathtaking danger after reading about the life of Jay Narzikul, a boy from Central Asia who avoided death traps of dictators and divulges secrets hidden by entire national governments or ignored by history.

FEDERALIST PAPERS AND ANTI-FEDERALISTS
Passionate debates about the nature of our government started at the time of drafting our *Constitution*. In these two books, leaders like Jay, Madison and Hamilton proposed a strong central power while critics like Patrick Henry worried about limits on taxation. Sound familiar? Read the beginning of national debate to understand today's discourse.

THAT'S RIGHT !!

MANY OF OUR AUTHORS ARE AVAILABLE FOR SPEAKING ENGAGEMENTS. CHECK IT OUT ON OUR WEBSITE OR EMAIL

www.pavilionpress.com
webmaster@pavilionpress.com